A NEW APPROACH

SECOND EDITION

Hinduism

Verc

A MEMBER OF THE HODDER HEADLINE GROUP

For my mother.

The Publishers would like to thank the following for permission to reproduce copyright material:

Photo credits

Archivo Iconografico, S.A./CORBIS: p. 79; Baldev/Corbis Sygma: p. 82 (left); BAPS Swaminarayan Sanstha (The Swaminarayan Hindu Mission): p. 85; David Bartruff/CORBIS: pp. 7 (right) and 99; Bridgeman (National Museum of India, New Delhi, India. Out of copyright.): p. 25; Radhika Chalasani/CORBIS: p. 74 (bottom); CIRCA/Robyn Beeche: p. 91 (left); CIRCA Photo Library/William Holtby: pp. 6, 17, 61 (bottom), 62 (both), 63, 72 and 94 (top); CIRCA/Bipin J. Mistry: pp. 15 and 48 (bottom); CIRCA/Ged Murray: pp. 47 and 64; CIRCA/John Smith: pp. 11 (top), 58, 66 (top), 68 and 94 (bottom); Sheldan Collins/CORBIS: p. 26; David Cumming/ Eye Ubiquitous/CORBIS: p. 52 (right); Michael Freeman/CORBIS: pp. 41 (bottom) and 76; Lindsay Hebberd/CORBIS: p. 53 (left), 55 (top) and 75; Historical Picture Archive/CORBIS: pp. 31, 40 and 41 (top); Robert Holmes/CORBIS: p. 67; Hulton Archive: p. 9; Hulton-Deutsch Collection/CORBIS: p. 82 (right); India Book House: p. 78 (bottom); Wolfgang Kaehler/CORBIS: p. 74 (top); Larry Lee Photography/CORBIS: p. 46 (top); Reuters/CORBIS: p. 61 (top); David Rose: p. 66 (bottom); Anders Ryman/CORBIS: p. 52 (left); Chuck Savage/CORBIS: p. 13; Janez Skok/CORBIS: p. 29 (right); Van Den Berge Robert/Corbis Sygma: p. 56 (bottom); Ajay Verma/Reuters/CORBIS: p. 65; Victoria and Albert Museum: p. 97 (left) (CT11656 IM.256-1921); Brian A. Vikander/CORBIS: p. 101; Veronica Voiels: pp. 3, 30, 53 (right), 73 (bottom), 91 (right & bottom) and 97 (right); World Religions Photo Library: pp. 2, 4, 5, 7 (left), 8 (both), 11 (bottom), 12 (both), 14, 16, 19, 20 (both), 28, 29 (left), 38, 39, 46 (bottom), 48 (top), 50, 54, 55 (bottom), 56 (top), 57, 71, 73 (top), 77, 78 (top) and 93.

Text acknowledgements

The Complete Works of Swami Vivekananda is published by Advaita Ashrama, (Calcutta: 1975). Gavid Flood, *An Introduction to Hinduism*, published by Cambridge University Press (1996). Quotes from the Bhagavad Gita adapted from *Bhagavad Gita As It Is* by A. C. Bhaktivedanta Swami Prabhupuda, Collier Macmillan (London: 1972), unless otherwise stated. *Ethical Issues in Six Religious Traditions*, edited by P. Morgan and C. Lawton, Edinburgh University Press (1996). All quotes from the Chandogya Upanishad and Rig Veda taken from *Hindu Scriptures* by R. C. Zaehner, Everymans Library (1966 and 1984), unless otherwise stated. *Interpreting Religious Hindus* by E. Wayne, J. Everington, D. Kadodwala and N. Nesbitt is published by Heinemann. Navajivan Publishing House (Ahmemdabad: 1969) for all quotes from *The Selected Works of Mahatma Gandhi*. All quotes from the Upanishads taken from *The Upanishads*, translation and introduction by Valerie S. Roebuck, Penguin Classics (2000), unless otherwise stated. *Hindu Scriptures*, edited with a new translation by Dominic Goodall, Phoenix Giant Paperback (1996). *The Legend of Krishna* by Nigel Frith is published by Sheldon Press (1975). *Explaining Hindu Dharma, A Teacher's Guide* by Dr N. K. Priaja (1999) is published by Vishwa Hindu Parishad (UK).

Every effort has been made to trace all copyright holders, but if any have been inadvertently overlooked the Publishers will be pleased to make the necessary arrangements at the first opportunity.

All artwork by Barking Dog Art.

Although every effort has been made to ensure that website addresses are correct at time of going to press, Hodder Murray cannot be held responsible for the content of any website mentioned in this book. It is sometimes possible to find a relocated web page by typing in the address of the home page for a website in the URL window of your browser.

Orders: please contact Bookpoint Ltd, 130 Milton Park, Abingdon, Oxon OX14 4SB. Telephone: (44) 01235 827720. Fax: (44) 01235 400454. Lines are open from 9.00–6.00, Monday to Saturday, with a 24-hour message answering service. Visit our website at www.hoddereducation.co.uk.

© Veronica Voiels 2005
First published in 2005 by
Hodder Murray, a member of the Hodder Headline Group
338 Euston Road
London NW1 3BH

Impression number 10 9 8 7 6 5 4 3 2 1
Year   2010 2009 2008 2007 2006 2005

Cover photo courtesy of Taxi/ Getty Images/ Justin Pumfrey.
Typeset in Berling 10.5pt by Fakenham Photosetting Limited, Fakenham, Norfolk.
Printed in Dubai.

A catalogue record for this title is available from the British Library

ISBN-10: 0 340 81504 3
ISBN-13: 9 780340 81504 5

Contents

UNIT ONE | Hinduism as a Way of Life

KEY WORDS

Ahimsa: non-violence or non-harm.
Ambedkar: an important Indian politician 1891–1956 who ensured that the dalits were given fair treatment.
Ashrama: stage in life.
Asteya: truthfulness and honesty.
Brahmin: priest/teacher.
Caste: social status, from birth.
Dalit: a person outside the caste system; untouchable.
Dharma: right conduct.
Dharma shastras: the rules, laws and customs that explain the duties for each stage of life.
Jatakarma: birth ceremony.
Jati: particular occupation or job.
Karma: law of cause and effect; destiny.
Kshatriya: warrior/ruler.
Moksha: final goal, when the soul is freed from the body and merges with god.
Mundan or Choodakarma: ceremony marking a child's first haircut.
Samskars: rites of passage that mark important stages in life; in Hinduism there are 16 samskars.
Sanatan dharma: eternal laws; universal principles of morality.
Satya: truth.
Sauca: purity.
Shraddha rites: special rituals conducted for departed relatives 12 days after their death.
Shudra: manual worker.
Upanayana: sacred thread ceremony for Hindu boys of higher castes during adolescence.
Vaishya: merchant; trader.
Varna: colour or caste.
Varnashramadharma: dharma rules and customs for each stage of life and each caste.
Vivaha: marriage ceremony.
Vivekànanda: a Hindu saint and reformer in the nineteenth century.

DHARMA

> Hinduism is the religion of the majority of people in India and Nepal, as well as being an important cultural force in all other continents of the world. Any visitor to India from the West is struck by the colour, sounds, smells and vibrancy of daily ritual observances, and by the centrality of religion in peoples' lives.
>
> Gavid Flood, *An Introduction to Hinduism*, page 1

The Hindu religion includes all aspects of life including daily routine, at home and at work, moral values, relationships with family members and friends, the natural world and the universe at large. This wonderful religion has existed for thousands of years and is deeply rooted in the history and culture of India. Some have said that it is necessary to know and appreciate Indian culture before a full understanding of Hinduism can be gained.

KEY QUESTION

Why is Hinduism a way of life?

'Hinduism is not a religion but more a way of life' is often stated by Hindus themselves. In the West, religion is sometimes separated from everyday life, such as work and home. However, Hindus believe that a person's beliefs affect all aspects of their behaviour and outlook on life – 'what you believe in affects the sort of person

▲ Anyone from the West who has travelled in India will comment on the crowded streets and chaotic traffic. There are often traffic jams in the holy city of Varanasi when all the visitors arrive. Bullock carts, cycle rickshaws, auto rickshaws and taxis jostle with holy men, pilgrims and street vendors.

you become'. This is very clearly understood and appreciated in Hinduism.

One central concept in Hinduism is **dharma**. The origin of the word in the Sanskrit language and ancient Vedic scriptures comes from the word 'Dhru', which means 'to hold and support', and the concept of 'Rta', which means 'harmony' and 'order' as opposed to destruction, disorder and chaos. Thus, dharma means that goodness and truth prevail in the world as opposed to evil and falsehood. In essence, dharma means goodness and truth.

What is the link between dharma and karma?

The concept of dharma is linked to the law of **karma**, or the law of cause and effect. This means that nothing happens by accident because everything has been caused by some action in the recent or distant past. So, good fortune such as a happy home and work life is due to good actions in this life or a previous life. Good deeds or moral actions will always have good results, and bad deeds and immoral actions will always have bad results. Also, a person's thoughts, words and deeds in the present will affect their future circumstances. So, Hindus believe it is very important to follow the rules and laws of dharma as this will help to ensure that their lives will be based in goodness and have good consequences for themselves and others. Dharma refers to all the laws and rules that must be followed by everyone to provide a happy, well ordered and harmonious world to live in. We call these rules and laws morality.

So how do Hindus follow the laws of dharma? They live their lives based on moral principles

A New Approach – Hinduism

which are expressed in **sanatan dharma**, and do good actions by following the duties for their stage in life and caste, called **varnashramadharma**.

Why is following dharma so important for Hindus?

Sanatan dharma means the eternal law or eternal religion. These are guiding principles of moral behaviour that apply to all people at all times, past and present.

This includes:

- non-harm or non-violence (**ahimsa**)
- truthfulness (**satya**)
- not stealing (**asteya**)
- purity of mind and body (**sauca**).

▲ In India, cows are allowed freedom to roam where they wish and are sometimes cared for by temple priests. They are considered to be sacred beasts, even deities, because of their ability to provide essential needs of life – nourishment of milk and cow dung for fuel.

> Having no ill feelings for any living being in all manners possible and for all times is called ahimsa.

The practice of ahimsa has always been very important in Hinduism and is expressed in a variety of ways, for example, by not harming or killing animals. The cow in particular is a sacred animal for Hindus. Mahatma Gandhi was a famous reformer in the twentieth century and is regarded by many Hindus as a saint who based his whole life upon this principle of non-violence and inspired many people in the West to solve their conflicts in a non-violent way.

PERSPECTIVES

Ahimsa means non-violence based on love for all living beings.

'It includes the whole of creation, not just humans. Ahimsa includes the whole of creation, all living beings, not just human beings. It is not non-violence if we merely love those that love us ... it is non-violence only when we love those that hate us. Ahimsa is an attribute of the brave. Cowardice and ahimsa do not go together any more than water or fire.'

The Selected Works of Mahatma Gandhi, Vol VI, page 153

TASK

Discuss why non-violence is a difficult principle to put into practice today.

KEY QUESTION

In what ways are **castes** similar and different to social classes in Britain today?

VARNASHRAMADHARMA

In answering the question 'Who am I?' a Hindu would refer to their caste and stage in life. Their caste (**varna**) is one of the four divisions of society, and their stage in life is one of the four stages or **ashramas**. So, a Hindu's sense of identity is formed by the caste they are born into and their stage of life, such as student, married or retired. The duties and responsibilities (dharma) for their caste (varna) and stage of life (ashrama) combine to form their varnashramadharma.

Karma and caste

Hindus believe that the caste a person is born into is the result of their previous actions according to the law of karma. If they live their life in a pure and moral way, do many generous deeds, fulfil their duties and develop a good character, then they are likely to be reborn in a higher caste. So by believing in the law of karma, some Hindus accept the caste they are born into and simply hope for a better caste in the next existence.

What are the social origins of caste?

All Hindus are born into a particular caste, which is revealed in the family name or surname, but what really matters to Hindus is their job or occupation within the caste system. This occupation or job is known as **jati**. As Indian society developed, the variety of occupations increased as each village required its potters, weavers, basket-makers, shoemakers, carpenters, etc. Jatis are these traditional occupations, which are passed on from father to son and become hereditary. Eventually, these occupations formed guilds or associations and only members of the same occupation were allowed to join.

They became like exclusive clubs in which only members of the same occupation were allowed to join.

In this way jatis developed into castes with rules forbidding marriage and dining between the different castes. These social rules became

▲ This woman is a laundrywoman. It is her jati, or family occupation. She has an essential role to play in village life. Her and her family will probably have been doing this kind of work for generations.

more and more detailed and fixed and now form the basis of caste customs observed today.

For many Hindus it is still very important to marry within the same caste. The higher castes are considered to be very pure and superior, and so to marry a person from a lower caste is considered to be lowering yourself to their level and so very degrading. Higher castes are meant to be very pure in their lives. This means cleanliness in every way including clean thoughts. So the higher castes are meant to avoid contact with the lower classes in case they become impure or polluted by contact with them. These ideas of purity and pollution can affect the ways in which people of different castes respond to each other.

A Hindu's caste status therefore affects their life in very important ways, such as:

- the kind of job they are trained in
- the people they dine or share food with, and
- the person they marry.

▲ This man is a cobbler. His work involves leather, and since contact with the skin of dead animals is particularly polluting, he is a Harijan (see page 6). No Hindu from a higher caste would consider doing this sort of work.

(see page 6)

PERSPECTIVES

Some of the beliefs and customs about caste are based in ancient scriptures known as 'The Laws of Manu'. This is a code of conduct for all castes and stages of life that was written some time between 200 BCE and 200 CE.

These scriptures are regarded as smriti, or wisdom that is remembered rather than heard. Some of the laws presented here seem very extreme and cruel by today's standards. **Ambedkar** quoted them in his writings and campaigns for the untouchables.

'All those tribes in the world, which are excluded from the community, born from the mouth, the arms, the thighs and the feet of the Brahman are called Dasyus (Dalit). Their dress shall be the garments of the dead, they shall eat their food from broken dishes, black iron shall be their ornaments, they must wander from place to place. A man who fulfils his religious duty shall not seek contact with them, their associations must be among themselves and they must only marry their equals. If one of these peoples intentionally defiles by his touching a member of the twice born caste he shall be put to death.'

Writings and speeches of Dr Ambedkar, page 90

Untouchables

Because some tasks were considered to be particularly unclean, especially those dealing with dead animals or rubbish, the people who dealt with them were considered to be so unclean as to be outside the caste system altogether and were called the untouchables or Dalits. Gandhi renamed Dalits as Harijans, which means 'Children of God', to ensure they were treated with the respect by all Hindus and to change their status in everyone's eyes.

VARNA

This term refers to the four main social groupings or classes in Hindu society. A person is born into the same caste or social group as their parents, and this caste is handed onto their children. This is what is meant by hereditary caste. It is impossible to move out of the caste you are born into. In the past, caste was very important in Hindu society, but today it is seen as out of date by modern Hindus. However, the idea still exists that some castes are higher and superior to others. In Hinduism there are considered to be four main castes:

1 **Brahmins** (priests)
2 **Kshatriyas** (warriors and rulers)
3 **Vaishyas** (traders)
4 **Shudras** (manual workers).

1 The Brahmins

The Brahmins are the priests and higher professions such as teachers and doctors. They have responsibility for preserving the traditions and rituals of Hinduism. They study and understand the Hindu teachings in the scriptures. They set a good moral example for others by remaining pure in words and deeds.

▲ This is a Brahmin family, engaged in a religious ritual outside their home. They have made a special altar with offerings and are reading out loud from the sacred scriptures.

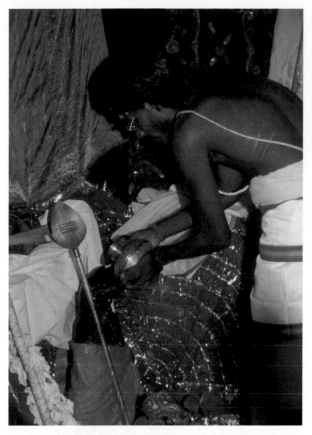

▲ A Brahmin priest at Tirupur, wearing his sacred thread. A Brahmin is considered to be pure in mind and body, and therefore the best person to make offerings to the deities. In this picture the priest is simply wearing a dhoti, and has cleansed his body.

▲ This man is a soldier and an officer, and is of the Kshatriya caste.

2 The Kshatriyas

The Kshatriyas are the rulers and military forces in society, such as the royal family, the prime minister and members of the government, and officers in the armed forces. They have responsibility for leadership, ruling society, making decisions about the general welfare of the people, and defending them from all forms of injustice and tyranny.

3 The Vaishyas

The Vaishyas are the business people in society dealing with money and commercial activities, such as directors of companies, bankers, financial advisers, solicitors, shop owners and traders. They have responsibility for providing the material goods and the wealth of society.

4 The Shudras

The Shudras are the workers and servants in society, such as farm labourers, factory workers, builders and manual workers. They have the responsibility for doing the physical and manual work and serving the needs of the other castes.

▲ This trader of spices is of the Vaishya caste.

▲ This man is a basket weaver. This is not just his occupation, but shows his place within the caste system. Baskets like this, which in the West are used mainly for decorative purposes, are essential for a whole variety of tasks in Indian village life.

TASK BOX

a) To what extent do you think your family background influences the choices you make about what to do in life?

b) In traditional Hindu society, everyone is born into a particular caste and that influences many aspects of a person's life. Make a list of the advantages and disadvantages you see in having your life influenced in that way.

c) If you could choose to be born into one of the four main castes, which one would it be and why?

Responses to caste in India and Britain today

Among Hindus today there are a variety of attitudes towards caste. In the more traditional way of life in the villages it is still quite a strong feature, because it helps to provide security and stability by giving everyone an essential role and function to play to keep village life running smoothly. Most villages have a caste council, which offers help and support to its members, and which functions rather like a social security system at grass-roots level.

However, Indian society is changing and becoming a developed and industrialised country, so traditional occupations are changing and new ones are developing. Life in the modern urban environments makes it difficult and irrelevant to observe caste customs. Discrimination on the grounds of caste is forbidden by Indian law. To ensure that lower castes are not disadvantaged in having a university education, special places are reserved for members of the lower castes and unscheduled castes (outcastes). There are countless examples of members of different castes choosing not to follow traditional occupations. One of the most famous of these was Ambedkar. He was a Dalit or untouchable, but became the most important member of the

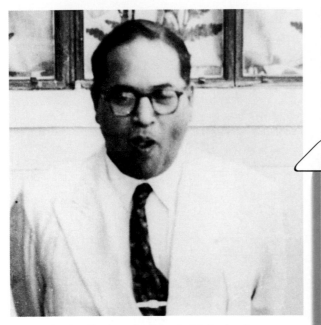

▲ Dr Ambedkar, an 'untouchable' who became the most important member of the Indian government during the gaining of India's independence.

by their experiences in the villages and cities of India. So, despite all the changes to Indian society and the presence of Hindu communities in all parts of the world, the issue of caste remains one in which a variety of views and opinions still exist.

Indian government at the time India was gaining its independence after the Second World War. He used his power and status to improve the conditions of the lower caste and untouchables, as well as ensuring that the 'untouchability' was outlawed by the Indian constitution. Many other reformers in Hinduism in the nineteenth and twentieth centuries, such as Gandhi and Swami **Vivekànanda**, also campaigned against some of the injustices of the caste system and 'untoucha-bility'. Many Hindus today would like to see the caste system die out.

One of the areas where caste distinctions are noticeable is in temple worship. In India, some temples are banned to those of lower castes. This is due the notions of purity and impurity associated with upper and lower castes. In Britain today, the issue of observing caste rules is often discussed among the local communities and temple councils. While most British temples are open to all castes there are some who want the caste distinctions to remain. For young Hindus who are born and brought up in Britain, the caste laws seem less important to them than the older generation whose outlook has been formed

TEST YOURSELF

1 What are the benefits of the caste system for village life in India?
2 How did the caste system develop in India?

TASK BOX

a) Discuss what is meant by sense of identity.
b) How do the following contribute to your sense of identity:
   (i)   parents?
   (ii) friends?
   (iii) the place you live?
   (iv) your social class?

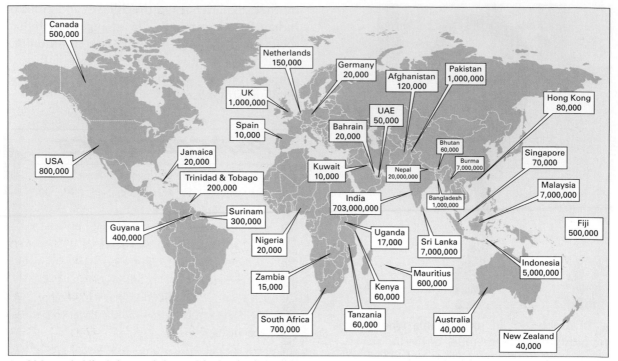

▲ Although Hinduism originated in India, it has spread throughout the world. This map shows countries in which there are 10,000 or more Hindus.

THE ASHRAMAS

KEY QUESTION

What are the four stages of life?

Just as each caste has its particular duty to follow, there is also dharma for the four ashramas or stages in life. These stages follow the natural process of growing up and growing old in society, but also recognise the importance of duties to society and the need to give attention to the spiritual and religious aspects of life. The ancient law books of Manu describe some of these four stages of life.

1 Brahmacharya or student stage

This begins with the initiation rite of the sacred thread called **upanayana**, which is performed only on boys in the three upper castes. In the past, this stage would involve studying the Vedic scriptures under the guidance of a specially chosen guru or priest. It would involve leaving the family home and living at the guru's special school (gurukula), traditionally in the forest or some secluded place. It was a life that involved service to the guru and his family, the practice of yoga, the study of scriptures, the arts and sciences and a life of simplicity, celibacy and self-discipline. On their departure after training, the guru would urge his pupils to speak only the truth, to never forget dharma, to serve elders, to remember the teachings of the Vedas and to regard their mother, father, teacher and guest as divine beings to be honoured and revered.

Nowadays, very few boys attend the traditional schools to study the scriptures, instead they attend the primary and secondary schools in their neighbourhood, but it is still regarded as a student's duty to gain knowledge through study, to show regard for teachers and parents and to learn the rules and rituals of the Hindu tradition.

▲ A traditional gurukala.

▲ Boys attend a scripture class.

2 Grihasta or householder

This begins when the student returns from his studies, marries and takes on the duties of a householder. This stage is considered to be very important as marriage is a sacred duty for Hindus in order to continue the family and all the social and religious obligations that go with it. The ritual of marriage is called **vivaha**, a word which also relates to maintaining order and harmony. No religious ritual can be performed by a man without his wife. No man's or woman's life is seen as complete without marriage. Householders are expected to give to charity, care for aged parents, offer hospitality to guests, and provide a settled, well-run household.

A married woman's duties include bringing up the children, managing the household expenses, preparing food, keeping the home clean and organising the celebration of festivals and other religious rites. Today, many Hindu woman have full-time jobs as well.

A husband must provide for his wife and children, educate and arrange marriages for his sons and daughters, earn money honestly and spend it on ways that are beneficial to himself and others.

◀ In the West, many people live in what is called a 'nuclear family' – mother, father and children all living together. There are also many single-parent families and people who choose to live on their own. Hinduism, by contrast, places great importance on the extended family with relatives of three or four generations living together. This photo shows three generations of a Gujerati family living together in London.

3 Vanaprastha or retirement stage

This stage occurs when the children are grown up and able to run their own lives, and when a grandson is born to ensure that the family will continue. The head of the household is then able to hand over responsibilities to his elder son. Vanaprastha refers to the retirement from daily work, which in ancient times was signified by becoming a forest dweller (this is what vanaprastha really means). The duties of this stage are to become detached from worldly goods and material concerns and devote time to quietness, solitude and the study of the scriptures and meditation. Those in this stage are seen as wise elders in the family and are called upon for advice and help in educating the children. Not all Hindus take on the particular duties of this stage but those who do are highly respected.

▲ Two elders help to distribute free rice at a temple festival.

4 Sannyasin or renunciation stage

This stage of life is especially noted in Hinduism. It requires the complete giving up of all worldly ties and possessions and devoting one's entire life to the spiritual goal of liberation or **moksha**. Some sannyasins become wandering holy men with no fixed abode and spend their whole life on pilgrimage in prayer, meditation and the study of the scriptures. Not many Hindus enter this stage but it is regarded very highly as a holy and spiritual way of life.

▲ This is a typical Indian sadhu (sannyasin) or wandering holy man. You can tell he is a sadhu by his mala beads and orange robe. He will have very few possessions, live in the space next to his shrine and depend on gifts from passers-by to sustain himself.

Underlying the particular duties of each caste and stage in life are four basic aims in life, which are also expressed in the law books of Manu.

The four aims in life are:

1 **dharma** – practising the right conduct in religious and social duties
2 **artha** – earning material wealth by honest means and providing for family and society
3 **kama** – enjoying the pleasures and beauty of life
4 **moksha** – aiming for the final goal of release from the round of rebirth and attaining liberation.

So, a Hindu who carries out all of his or her religious and moral duties according to their stage in life, caste, occupation and financial means is said to be true to his or her dharma.

▲ Gaining wealth by honest means is a valid goal in life for Hindus. This businessman looks particularly pleased with himself!

TASK BOX

a) What do you think the purpose of the student stage is in the Hindu tradition?
b) In what way is the brahmacharya the same or different from the student stage among young people in Britain?
c) Do you agree with the view that marriage should be a sacred duty?
d) What is the Hindu attitude towards old age and what do you think of this attitude?
e) It is sometimes said that Hindus have a strong sense of duty. If many people had a strong sense of duty how would this affect family life and the wider society?

RITES OF PASSAGE

KEY QUESTION

Why do all cultures like to have a special ceremony to mark certain stages in life?

Rites of passage are special rituals that mark a transition from one stage of life to another. These stages of birth, becoming an adult, getting married and death are deeply emotional as well as socially important. Thus they are celebrated with special actions and social or public gatherings of families and communities. So important are these stages that they are given religious and spiritual expression through rituals and sacraments. Hindus have a great variety of rites of passage, called **samskars**. This word is most accurately translated as 'sacraments', as the purpose is to sanctify, purify and safeguard the passage from one stage of life to the next. There are 16 samskars in Hinduism and they are a kind of religious duty in the ancient Law Books of Manu or the **Dharma shastras**. Not all 16 samskars may be fully practised, but they will be recognised in some way.

The most important of these are:

- birth and naming ceremonies
- sacred thread ceremony
- marriage rites
- death rites.

▲ This Hindu wedding is taking place in a Tamil temple in south-west London. Notice the special canopy in the background.

The 16 samskars consist of the following:

1 Conception of a child (Garbhahana). This is a ceremony performed at the first menstruation of the new bride to wish for the conception and fertilisation of an embryo (garbha) and the continuation of the human race.

2 **and** 3 Special rituals performed during pregnancy, at the second or third month and then at the sixth or eighth month to ensure the healthy development of the baby.

4 Birth ceremony (**Jatakarma**).

5 Naming ceremony (Namakarana).

6 Child's first outing (Nishkramana) at four months old.

7 Child's first solid food (Annaprashana).

8 Child's first haircut at 1–3 years (**Mundan** or **Choodakarma**). This is seen as a kind of purifying ceremony removing the impurities of being born, as well as the karma of a previous life.

9 Child's ears are pierced.

10 The sacred thread ceremony (Upanayana). This is the initiation of boys from the three upper castes into the student stage of life.

11 The start of formal education (Vedarambha).

12 Graduation from studies (Samavartana).

13 Marriage (Vivaha).

14 Retirement (Vanaprastha), usually around the age of 60.

15 Withdrawing from worldly concerns and becoming a holy man (Sannyasa). Supposed to be at the age of 75 but may be earlier or later than this.

16 Death rites (Antyeshti). This will also include **Shraddha** ceremonies, in which respects are paid to departed relatives.

Birth and naming ceremonies

When a baby is born it is welcomed into the world with a short ceremony. Sometimes the family priest is invited to carry out a ritual cleansing, so he will recite prayers and hymns from the scriptures and sprinkle the mother and baby with drops of water. In some families, when the father holds the baby for the first time he will dip a gold jewel into a mixture of ghee and honey and touch the lips of the baby with it. He asks for God's protection and whispers a prayer in its ear. 'May God the creator of all things grant you wisdom. Knowledge and wisdom are the sources of power and long life.'

Six to twelve days after the birth, the naming ceremony (Namakarana) will take place. On this day the mother may bathe for the first time after giving birth. She will be given new clothes and the house will be filled with fresh flowers. The father, who must not have shaved since the baby was born, will now remove his growth of hair, in order to emphasise the sense of removal of pollution and the birth of new life. The family priest may conduct the ritual and cast a horoscope to determine what the first letter of the baby's

A New Approach – Hinduism

name should be. Rice grains are spread on a metal plate, which is kept in front of the couple. The father, using a gold ring or piece of gold wire, writes the name of the family deity, followed by the date of the birth of the child and the proposed name. The father whispers the name into the baby's right ear. The names always have an important meaning and may be associated with gods and goddesses or with the powers of nature.

Girl's name	Meaning
Anvi	Earth
Padma	flower
Usha	dawn
Asha	hope
Chandra	moon
Hetal	friendly
Hema	golden
Tejal	brightness

Parvati, Savita and Anusuya are linked to the names of the goddesses.

Boy's name	Meaning
Anand	happy
Amit	lovable
Aakash	sky
Bimal	pure
Pankaj	lotus
Vijay	victory
Rajiv	lotus
Deepak	light

Mahesh, Jagdish and Niranjan are linked to the names of the gods.

The scriptures recommend that boys' names should be of two or four syllables while girls' should be of one, three or five syllables. In ancient times male names were suffixed by caste names, e.g. Sharma for Brahmins, Varma for Kshatriyas, Gupta for Vaishyas and Dasa for Shudras. However, in modern times such suffixes do not necessarily indicate varna or jati.

▲ A Hindu priest prepares a horoscope for a naming ceremony.

The sacred thread ceremony

Most religions have special ceremonies to mark the transition to adulthood and commitment to a particular faith or religion. In Hinduism, the most important ceremony for the upper three castes is the sacred thread ceremony. Members of the Brahmin, Kshatriya and Vaishya castes are known as twice born and to enter fully into their caste they have to be initiated with the Upanayana rite. In this samskar the boy is introduced to the guru or teacher and given the sacred thread (Yajnopaveet), which consists of three strands. These symbolise the three vows or promises that the young adult will have to observe and follow in his life. These are:

- the duty to promote knowledge gained from all sages, thinkers and scientists
- the duty to look after and respect one's parents and ancestors
- the duty towards the society and nation in which one lives.

It is also an initiation into the student stage (brahmacharya) and is usually undertaken for boys between the ages of eight and sixteen. It marks the boy's coming of age when he needs to understand the importance of belonging to the Hindu community and also to begin his formal education and learning of Hindu scriptures. In the past, the boy left home to receive his education from a guru or spiritual teacher where he would have learnt meditation and the language of Sanskrit and teachings of the Vedas. This is not the case today but this stage of life does require the young adult to observe celibacy and moral purity. It is a religious and a social occasion and is performed in front of family and friends. In this ceremony the boy passes from the care and authority of his mother and comes under the influence of the male members of the family. Because of a move towards more equality between sexes, many Hindus now feel that both boys and girls should undergo this samskar.

▲ This photo shows the changing of the sacred thread – a ceremony which takes place annually in September.

The ceremony

The best day for the ceremony is usually chosen by the family priest or astrologer. The boy's head is shaved, except for a tuft of hair on the crown. He takes a bath and wears a special white dhoti. The boy and his mother share a special meal together, then the mother leaves the proceedings. The boy then stands facing west, opposite his father who faces east. A piece of cloth is held between father and son and songs of blessings are sung. The priest conducts a special sacred fire ritual called homa. Offerings of rice and ghee are made to Agni, the god of fire. The boy is given new clothes and a loop of soft cotton is placed around his neck. Then a loop of white cotton made from three strands is placed over the boy's left shoulder so that it hangs diagonally across his chest and under his right arm and is tied with a spiritual knot. The father says, 'May this sacred thread destroy my ignorance, grant me long life and increase my understanding'. The boy repeats these words as he puts on the sacred thread. It is worn day and night for the rest of his life and is renewed annually at a special ceremony in September, which is called Ganesha Chaturti, Ganesha's birthday. The boy kneels on his right knee in front of his father or teacher and asks to be taught the Gayatri hymn which is recited to him. The boy then takes a vow of celibacy and makes promises to obey his father, teacher and the family priest and to concentrate on his studies. He is given a staff to enable him to follow the right path in his studies and pretends to leave home, but is persuaded to stay for the feast and presents from his family and friends.

Discuss what you think the effect of the sacred thread ceremony might be on the young Hindu's outlook on life and relationships with the rest of his family.

TEST YOURSELF

A B C

What are the main features of the:
i) birthing ceremony?
ii) sacred thread ceremony?

Marriage rites

In Hinduism, marriage is considered to be holy and a religious duty. It is not only the union between two partners, but an alliance between two families, so it is usually an arranged marriage. Once the choice has been made, a priest looks up the prospective partners' horoscopes to see how well their personality and temperament will suit each other, and to find a good time for the wedding. In India it would take place at the bride's home, in Britain a hall would be booked and large numbers of relatives would be prepared to travel great distances to attend. The wedding is often a costly affair for the bride's family because

▲ The photograph shows an extended family, who have gathered to have their photo taken in front of the Neasden temple in London.

her father will probably have agreed to give a dowry to her husband. A dowry is a usually a large sum of money given to the groom by the bride's father to set them up in married life. Although this is now an illegal practice it is still sometimes observed as a matter of pride.

The ceremony

1 The bridegroom and his family are welcomed at the bride's house. Members of both families are introduced. The bridegroom is brought to a specially decorated altar called a 'Mandap', offered a seat and a welcoming drink, which is a mixture of milk, ghee, yoghurt and honey.

2 Songs of blessings. The bride and groom stand facing each other. A silk cloth is held between them by the priest and his assistant to form a curtain. Rice grains are distributed among the guests. Songs of blessings are sung and the guests shower the couple with rice.

3 The daughter is given in marriage by her father to the groom who puts his daughter's right hand into the hand of her future husband. Her father asks the groom to promise to be moderate in the observance of his moral duty (dharma), the earning of money (artha) and the enjoyment of good things in life (kama).

4 Symbolic exchange of gifts. Prior to the exchange of gifts, a single cotton thread rubbed in turmeric is tied separately around each of the couple's wrists as a symbol that they are now bound for life. The groom's mother then gives an auspicious necklace (Mangala sootra) to the bride.

5 The sacred fire is lit and the priest recites the sacred mantras in Sanskrit. He invites the groom to make offerings to the fire as certain prayers are said. The bride shares in this act by touching his shoulder. The groom says to the bride:

I am the Sun you are the Earth. May my seed be planted in you to produce children. May they outlive us. May we love and admire one another and protect each other with a kind heart. May we see, hear and live hundred autumns.

I free this bride from the obligations to her father's family. Now she stands securely bound to her husband. May we be blessed with worthy offspring.

The end of the bride's sari that hangs over her shoulder is then tied to the scarf that her groom is wearing.

6 The taking of vows. The husband, holding his wife's hands, says: 'I hold your hand in the spirit of dharma we are both husband and wife.' The couple offer roasted rice to the sacred fire.

7 The bride steps onto a stone, which symbolises a rock and her willingness and strength to overcome difficulties in pursuit of her duties. Both walk gently around the sacred fire seven times holding hands, the bride leading three times, the groom leading four times. The bride's brothers pour barley in to the couple's hands, to be offered to the fire and to symbolise that they will all work jointly together for the welfare of society. The husband marks the parting of his wife's hair with red kum-kum powder for the first time. It is called soodar and is a sign of a married woman.

8 The seven steps. This is the main part of the ceremony. The couple walk seven steps around the sacred fire reciting a prayer at each step:
the first for food
the second for power
the third for prosperity
the fourth for happiness
the fifth for children
the sixth for health
the seventh for friendship.

9 Viewing the Pole Star. If the wedding is during the day, the couple look at the sun (Surya Darshan) in order to be blessed, and if it is at night they look in the direction of the Pole Star and the wife resolves to be unshaken and steadfast like the star.
The Pole Star is Dhruva, constant. May I be Dhruva in my husband's family.

10 The blessings. The couple are blessed by the elders and the priest for a long and prosperous married life.

This will be followed by a sumptuous feast to impress all the guests. When the bride enters the house of her husband's family for the first time she has one more ceremony to perform. She must kick over a metal pot containing wheat with her right foot so that the grain spilt over the threshold shows she will bring prosperity.

▲ The bride at a Rajasthani wedding where the women traditionally wear beautifully decorated and brightly coloured clothes. In this photo you see a young bride who has been garlanded and specially made up by her female relatives to look like a queen or goddess. The gold jewellery is her dowry for her husband.

TASK

a) In what way can marriage be seen as a religious duty?
b) How does the ceremony show the linking of two families as well as the union of two people?

Death rites

There are various death rites, which vary from region to region and family to family, although there are some common features, especially cremation. In Indian towns and cities, special cremation grounds stand ready for use and in the villages there is an area of land set aside for no other purpose. In Britain, Hindus cremate their dead at the local crematoria. In India, the nearest male relative conducts the funeral rites with the help of their family and local priest. All family members are closely involved in these last rites.

If the person who has died is a man, close male relatives bathe his body and dress him in new clothes. Female relatives do the same if the dead person is a woman. A funeral pyre is made of wood and sandalwood; saffron, musk and camphor are added to this to make it sweet smelling. This pyre may be carried to the nearest cremation ground in a kind of procession. As they approach the ground they may say, 'Ram's name is the name of truth. Such is the fate of all men.' The body is laid on a pile of wood then more wood is piled on top of the body. Ghee is put among the sticks to ensure that it will burn well and act as a purifying agent. The body is placed with its feet facing south towards the realm of the god of death, Yama. The son or chief mourner, instructed by the priest and other relatives, will light the pyre first at the north and then other parts. When it alights, nuts, rice and other offerings are thrown into the flames. One of the prayers chanted by the priest will include the following words:

> After death may the sun absorb your power of sight,
> The breath of the winds carry your soul,
> May you enter the shining levels as your karma permits.
> May all that is water return to the oceans.
> And your body return to the soil and be one with the earth.

▲ This is a rare photograph that shows the family washing the body before cremation in Pashupatinath.

Shraddha rites are associated with rites for the dead. These are part of the religious duties for Hindus prescribed in the ancient law books. The Shraddha ceremony is the annual homage paid to departed ancestors. The first one is performed at a holy place and thereafter at home. Each invited Brahmin represents a departed ancestor and many families commemorate all departed ancestors on the same day and these Brahmins are fed by the relatives.

▲ This is the last stage of a Hindu funeral when the ashes are floated in the river.

The funeral party remains until the fire begins to subside and it is clear that the deceased body has been consumed. After the funeral the mourners will bathe and change their clothes. Two or three days afterwards, the son comes back to the cremation ground to collect the ashes, which will later be scattered on a river or kept until they can be taken to the most sacred river, the Ganges. The mourning period lasts for ten days. It is not encouraged to show too much grief because it is believed that the deceased is passing on to another life and the soul is getting nearer to its final destination.

TASK

'These rites of passage (samskars) are more important as family gatherings than religious rituals.'
How far do you agree with this statement? What is the real purpose of these rituals?

1 What are the main actions performed at (i) a Hindu marriage and (ii) a Hindu cremation?

2 What is the purpose of the four rites of passage – birth, sacred thread ceremony, marriage and death?

3 Why do you think Hindus have 16 samskars?

4 In what ways are:
i) the birth of a child in a family
ii) becoming an adult at 18
iii) getting married
iv) death
the end of one life and the start of a new life?

---

1 a) What is the meaning of varnashramadharma for Hindus?　　　(4 marks)

b) State the main duties of each of the following stages of life:
- brahmacharya
- grihasta
- vanaprastha
- sannyasin.　　　(8 marks)

c) 'Hindus have to obey so many rules and perform so many duties that they do not have any individual freedom.'

Do you agree or disagree with the statement? Give reasons for your answer showing you have considered more than one point of view. (5 marks)

2 a) Why might a Hindu believe it is important to fulfil his dharma?　(5 marks)

b) Read the passage below carefully:

When they divided primal man
Into how many parts did they divide him?
What was his mouth? What his arms?
What are his thighs called? What his feet?

The Brahmin was his mouth,
His arms were made the Prince,
His thighs the common people
And from his feet the shudra were born.　　　(Rig Veda X, xc: 11–12.)

What does this hymn say about:
(i) the origin of the caste system?
(ii) the duties of Brahmins and Kshatriya?
(iii) why some castes are higher than others?　　　(9 marks)

c) 'The caste system is still an important feature of the Hindu community in India.' Do you agree or disagree with this statement? Give reasons for your answer showing you have considered more than one point of view.
　　　(5 marks)

Assignment

REMEMBER

- Dharma refers to the conduct that must be followed to create a harmonious world to live in.
- By following the right conduct (dharma) in this life, you will reap the rewards in the next life (karma).
- Dharma rules for each stage of life and caste (Varnashramdharma).
- The principles of Sanatan dharma: Non-harm, truthfulness, not stealing, and purity of mind and body.
- The caste a person is born into depends on their previous actions according to the laws of karma.

- A Hindu's occupation within their caste is known as jati.
- There are four main castes: Brahmins (includes priests and higher professions), Kshatriyas (includes rulers and military men), Vaishas (includes business people), and Shudras (includes servants and manual workers).
- The four main stages in life are: bharmacharya (student), grihasta (householder), vanaprasta (retirement), sannyasin (renunciation).
- The four aims in life are: dharma (duty), artha (wealth), kama (pleasure) and moksha (release from rebirth).

a) From the websites below find out as much as you can about the ceremonies of childhood besides the obvious ones of birth and naming. What do Hindus do at these times and why do they celebrate these stages?

b) Find out more about rituals for the dead and write about how they might help the family with their grief.

Dharma

- http://www.bbc.co.uk/ worldservice/people/features/world _religions/hinduism_prac.shtml
- http://www.pearls.org
  Search for 'Hinduism'.
- http://www.bbc.co.uk/religion/ religions/hinduism/index.shtml
- http://www.hinduism.fsnet.co.uk/ schools1.htm
- http://www.iskcon.org.uk/ies/ index.html
  Look for 'A brief summary of Hinduism'.
- http://www.hindunet.org/introduction/ index.htm
  Look for definitions of 'Hindu Dharma'.
- http://www.bbc.co.uk/schools/ gcsebitesize/re/

Rites of passage

- http://www.hindunet.org/introduction /index.htm
  Find out about marriage customs, the ceremony, finding a partner, etc.
- http://www.bbc.co.uk/religion/ religions/hinduism/features/rites/ weddings2.shtml
  Find out about a real Hindu wedding!
- http://dying.about.com
  Find out about Hindu views on death and dying and the rites of passage.
- http://dying.about.com
  Also discover an insider's view. An article about a son who 'prepares his father for heaven' through the Hindu funeral service.

WEBLINKS

2

KEY WORDS

Ananta: a huge sea serpent with many heads arising out of the ocean upon which Vishnu lies.

Atman: the inner spirit dwelling in every living being, including animals; it is the eternal, indestructible and perfect spirit in everyone.

Avatar: a god in human or animal form.

Bhagavad Gita: an important and popular scripture for Hindus, which explains why god came to earth in the form of Krishna.

Bhagavad Purana: stories about the main popular gods.

Bhakti: worshipping god with much love and often lots of singing and dancing.

Brahma: the creator god.

Brahman: the Hindu word for God, the ultimate being or life force and energy that creates the universe.

Chakra: wheel or disc.

Deity: one of the many gods worshipped by Hindus.

Devas: minor gods or spirits that inhabit the natural world, rivers, trees – even a human being can become like a deva or perfect being; devas are often goddesses.

Ganesha: an elephant-headed god who brings good luck.

Gopis: the milkmaids who worshipped Krishna.

Hanuman: divine powers in the form of the King of the Monkeys. As Rama's loyal and devoted companion he is sometimes worshipped as a god in his own right.

Krishna: one of the most popular avatars of Vishnu who loves human beings.

Lingum: the male sex organ; sometimes used as symbol for Shiva.

Maha Yogi: Shiva represented in human form.

Mantra: a repeated phrase or prayer used in religious rituals and meditation aimed at focusing the mind on god.

Meditation: the practice of stilling the mind and removing ordinary thoughts, developing deep concentration and wisdom through the power of the mind.

Nataraja: lord of the dance and another name for Shiva.

Om: a sacred sound that represents the powers of Brahman or God; the symbol of Hinduism.

Radha: Krishna's most devoted follower and wife.

Rama: another avatar of Vishnu who shows courage and goodness.

Rig Veda: one of the books of the Vedas, the most ancient hymns of the Aryan tribes of India.

Sanskrit: the ancient language in which the Vedas are written.

Shiva: the destroyer and re-creator god.

Trimurti: the three aspects of the ultimate being Brahman expressed as Brahma, Vishnu and Shiva; in other words three aspects of God in one God.

Vedas: some of the oldest sacred scriptures of India.

Vishnu: the preserver god.

▲ One God: many forms.

For Hindus there is no difficulty in accepting that there is one true God, which has many forms. The scriptures often state that God is one God that has many different forms, as this famous story illustrates.

Hindus believe:

A Hindu child asked her grandmother:
'Grandmother, how many gods are there?'
'There are as many gods as there are creatures, so there must be 300,000,000 gods.'
'Grandmother, how many gods are there, really?'
'3000 my child.'
'Grandmother, how many gods are there, really?'
'300 my child.'
'Grandmother, how many gods are there, really?'
'30 my child.'
'Grandmother, how many gods are there, really?'
'3 my child.'
'Grandmother, how many gods are there, really?'
'One my child, really.'

- there is one universal spirit called **Brahman**, which pervades the whole universe and is symbolised in the syllable **Om**.
- there are three main aspects of Brahman expressed in the **trimurti** – **Brahma** the creator, **Vishnu** the preserver and **Shiva** the destroyer
- in human and animal forms of Vishnu, most especially **Krishna** and **Rama**
- that lesser gods or **devas** are special to particular places, such as village deities and devas
- that God is present in all life-giving things like the cow, rivers and trees
- that God dwells in all creatures as the innermost spirit or true self.

The Hindu idea of the nature of God is expressed in many varied ways because Hinduism is one of the most ancient world religions. The origins of the Hindu idea of God goes so far back in time that the earliest evidence we have comes from the Indus Valley in 2000 BCE. Some clay tablets have drawings that show gods as male and female. Some scholars say that a famous clay tablet showing a horned **deity** sitting in a **meditation** posture with corn growing out of his chest is an early form of the god Shiva.

In the ancient **Rig Veda** hymns composed around 1500 BCE, God is seen as the power within the natural forces of thunder and lightning, the sun, the sky, the dawn, the earth and the moon. Later on, the priests and hymnwriters formed the idea that these powerful forces were different aspects of one supreme power. This idea is expressed in this famous verse from the Rig Veda.

They call him Indra, Mitra, Varuna, Agni and the heavenly nobly-winged Garatman. To what is one, sages give many a title. Thus God is One, but wise men call it by different names.

Rig Veda I.164, verse 46 (A Source Book in Indian Philosophy, page 21)

This idea that God is One but is known and worshipped in many different ways is the key to understanding the Hindu idea of God.

TASK

Why do you think Hindus appear to worship so many gods and yet believe in one God?

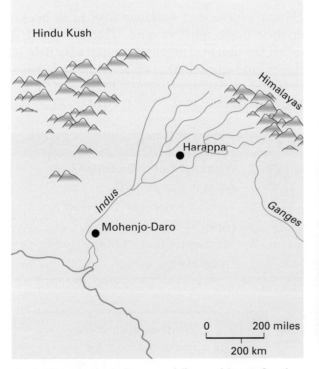

▲ Archaeological sites providing evidence for the Indus valley civilisation.

▲ This clay tablet probably shows an early form of the god Shiva. Although it may be almost 4000 years old, the same sitting position is still used in meditation. Notice how the god is linked with the idea of fertility – something which continues in the worship of Shiva today.

The meaning of Brahman

The word 'Brahman' has its origin in the early scriptures of Hinduism. It comes from the root 'brh', which means giving forth or growth and creation. Later on, it came to mean the life-giving power within the universe. In the scriptures known as the Upanishads, Brahman is sometimes described in personal terms as 'He', other times in impersonal terms as 'it'. The Upanishads say that this power dwells within all living beings in the universe and is also beyond the universe. It is a mysterious truth to grasp and the writers of these scriptures tried to express it in poetry and imagery.

> This whole universe is Brahman.
> Let a man revere it in all tranquillity as that from which all things are born and into which they dissolve and in which they breathe and move.
>
> *Chandogya Upanishad, Book III, Chapter XIV, verse 1*

▲ Brahman is believed to be everywhere and in everything – the origin of all that comes into being, including the light of a new day.

> Invisible, intangible, having neither family nor caste.
> Devoid of eye and ear, devoid of hands and feet
> Eternal, all pervading, penetrating everywhere, most subtle and changeless,
> The womb and origin of all that comes into being.
>
> *Mundaka Upanishad, Chapter 1, section 1, verse vi*
>
> He who consists of mind, whose body is the breath of life, whose form is light, whose idea is the real, whole self is space ... who encompasses all this universe, who does not speak and has no care, he is my self within the heart ... This my self within the heart is that Brahman.
>
> *Chandogya Upanishad, Book III, Chapter XIV, verse 3–5*

The meaning of Atman

Hindus believe that Brahman lives in all beings in their inner spirit or soul. This inner self is called the **atman**. The atman is like a particle of the cosmic spirit Brahman. It is the indestructible and eternal spirit, which lives on after the body has died.

TEST YOURSELF

1 Who or what is Brahman?
2 What is the atman?
3 'Hindus believe in one God'. True/False
4 'Hindus believe in many gods'. True/False

TASK

What do each of the quotations from the Upanishads reveal about the nature of and powers of Brahman?

THE SACRED SYMBOLS

The OM symbol

This symbol, consisting of three sounds, A-U-M, represents Hinduism and is always seen in temples and shrines. It is considered to be the sacred sound or vibration that is made by the life-giving power of the universe or Brahman. The three sounds are a **mantra** or a kind of prayer which, when uttered with reverence and faith, puts the person in touch with their inner nature and with God.

It represents:

- past, present and future
- birth, life and death
- Brahma, Vishnu and Shiva.

 The syllable (aksara) OM is all this: To explain further: What is called past, present and future is all just OM. Whatever else there is, beyond the three times, that too is all just OM.
Vaisvanara, whose state is waking, is the 'a'
Taijasa, whose state is dream, is the 'u'
Prajna, whose state is deep sleep, is the 'm'
So OM is the self. The one who knows this by self enters the self: The one who knows this.

Mandukya Upanishad, Verse 1, 9–12

The swastika symbol

This symbol is often found on Hindu temples or drawn as a pattern in the ground on coloured chalks. It is a sacred symbol to Hindus as it refers to the wheel of life, the life-giving powers of the sun, and being blessed with good fortune. However, it is often misunderstood by people in the West as it was used by the Nazi Party of Germany and is associated with their cruelty in the Second World War.

TEST YOURSELF

[A][B][C] What are the meanings of the OM and swastika symbols?

TASK BOX

a) Find a symbol that is used in everyday life, in shops, advertising, sport or transport. What is the message of the symbol? Why are symbols helpful to us?

b) What kind of religious symbols can you find? Why are they useful to believers and others? Why do we find symbols in religion?

c) Carefully draw the OM symbol and the swastika symbol. What Hindu beliefs are expressed in these symbols?

d) What does the concept of Brahman and the OM symbol reveal about the Hindu understanding of God?

WHAT IS THE HINDU TRIMURTI?

The Hindu trimurti refers to the three main gods of Hinduism. Brahma is the creator god, Vishnu the preserver god and Shiva the destroyer and re-creator god.

These are the three different purposes of Brahman's powers:

- to create the universe including planet Earth with all its living beings
- to keep the universe going
- to destroy the world in order to re-create it.

▲ This statue, called the trimurti because it shows three gods in one, represents Brahma, Vishnu and Shiva.

At first glance the images of the gods appear bewildering and part of a fantasy world, but as one investigates the meaning of the symbols and images it is possible to understand and appreciate the purpose and meaning of these gods for Hindus.

The images and pictures of these gods are often richly decorated and embellished. They always have several arms to indicate their many powers and in each hand they hold objects that show their particular powers. Colour is also used to symbolise their unique nature. These gods are accompanied by animals or birds, which are their special protectors, and vehicles to enable them to move around the cosmos. These symbols help worshippers to understand and relate to their chosen god and call upon their special powers.

Brahma

Brahma the creator god is shown with four heads facing in four different directions, symbolising that he has created the entire universe. He meditates in order to create the universe and he is guided by the Vedas, which he holds in one of his hands. The water pot or vessel held in another hand is used in the ritual of prayer prior to meditation, and is used by holy men who have chosen to withdraw from the world in order to develop and direct their spiritual nature. The rosary or mala beads, which he also holds, are used as an aid to meditation. He sometimes sits on a lotus, which is a symbol of purity as it emerges white and pure in the sunlight, untouched by the mud and slime out of which it emerges. He may also sit in the meditation posture to show he is not disturbed at all by the world around him.

Shiva

Shiva is the aspect of Brahman that destroys and re-creates the universe and he is shown in several different forms:

1 The lord of the dance or **Nataraja**.
2 The great Yogi or **Maha Yogi**.
3 The **lingum.**

▲ **This is an image of Shiva Nataraja, the lord of the dance.**

As Natararja, lord of the dance, Shiva is showing his energy and power in bringing the world into existence and then destroying it. He does this by dancing on the demon dwarf, which represents human pride and ignorance. This needs to be crushed if progress on the spiritual path is to be made.

The picture shows that in his hands he holds various objects, that may include:

■ an hourglass-shaped rattle drum (the damaru), which represents the rhythm of the universe that he controls
■ a deer, which represents an unsteady mind that jumps from one thing to another rather than settling on God
■ flames that symbolise his powers of destruction.

With his other hand he is making symbolic gestures or mudras, which convey a message. The upraised hand is saying, 'Do not fear I will protect as I destroy'. The hand indicating the demon points to the destruction of ignorance. His trailing locks of hair show the frenzy of this dance as his energy swirls about the world. He is also surrounded by a circle of fire that expresses the eternal motion of the universe in the process of creation, destruction and re-creation.

▲ Shiva as Maha Yogi (see page 30).

Shiva as **Maha Yogi** (see the picture on page 29) is represented in a human form seated in a meditation posture, often set against a white background of the snowy Himalayas. These represent the purity of his mind, which is not distracted by the world as he sits in deep meditation. His posture represents the perfect harmony and serenity of a person's mind when it has gained final peace and freedom through deep meditation. His half-closed eyes show that his mind is focused on his inner self and the presence of God within himself. He has a pile of tangled hair in a top knot rising in a cone on his head, out of which pours the river Ganges next to the crescent moon. This relates to a story in which the river Ganges in its descent to Earth would have destroyed and shattered the earth had Shiva not caught it in his locks of hair. The crescent moon indicates the coolness and calmness of a yogi in meditation. His third eye situated in the middle of his forehead signifies his powers of concentration and the wisdom and special insight developed by all yogis and

▲ This is a Shiva lingum outside the eighteenth-century temple at Grishneshwar, north of Aurangabad.

especially the great yogi, Shiva. His complexion is blue, relating to another story in which he drank poison in order to save the world from being destroyed by evil. Blue also symbolises the infinity of the sky and the oceans. He is often draped by a tiger skin, which symbolises the need to overcome arrogant pride and Shiva's power to destroy the enemies of evil and ignorance. Similarly, the serpent coiled around his neck or body shows his powers to control his desires and ego. He holds the trident, which is a sign of a holy man, a symbol of asceticism or withdrawing from the pleasures of worldly life.

Shiva as represented in the lingum (below left) is a symbol of Shiva's energy and power to generate and regenerate life. In some of the myths, Shiva's lingum or phallus is described as a cosmic pillar reaching into space at one end and into the centre of the earth at the other. Thus it represents cosmic power and light. It is in this form that Shiva is often shown in shrines and temples. In these temples Shiva's vehicle, Nandi the bull, is the protector of the god and the doorkeeper of the temple.

Vishnu

Vishnu comes from a word meaning 'all-pervading', which means his presence is everywhere. His function in the Hindu triad of gods is to maintain and preserve the order and harmony of the universe. He is shown lying on a many-headed cobra (**ananta**), which symbolises cosmic energy and cosmic time. Vishnu arises out of an ocean of milk, which symbolises endless bliss and endless mind. His colour is blue to indicate he is as infinite and as endless as the sky.

In one of his four hands he holds the discus or **chakra** to show he maintains the order and righteousness in the universe. In another hand he holds the conch shell (**shanha**) which, because of the deep humming sound it makes when held next to the ear, denotes the music of the cosmos, calling people to lead a pure and spiritual life. He also holds the mace and wears a crown to indicate his kingly authority and ability to protect the world and remove evil from it. He is sometimes shown sitting on a lotus, which is a symbol of the beauty and purity of the universe.

A New Approach – Hinduism

His vehicle is Garuda, a man-eagle, which is a symbol of strength, power and piety. All the symbols of Vishnu are intended to remind the worshipper of the need to follow religious and moral laws and to prevent suffering and disaster from taking over the world.

Vichnou.

▲ A lithograph of Vishnu on a throne.

TEST YOURSELF

A **B** **C** What are the different functions of Brahma, Vishnu and Shiva?

TASK

Draw a picture of Brahma, Vishnu and Shiva and label your pictures with the symbolic meaning of their postures.

KEY QUESTION

What different forms does the goddess take?

THE GODDESS

In Hinduism the goddess is very important and is widely worshipped in India in a variety of forms. The scriptures refer to the goddess as the creative energy shakti, which is the power that breathes life into things in the human and natural world. Without the energy and power of shakti, the male gods would have no power. Shakti is like the yeast that is added to bread, it brings all the other ingredients to life. So, without the creative energy of shakti the universe would not be full of life. Shakti takes many different forms in the various goddesses worshipped by Hindus.

Parvati

She is the consort or wife of Shiva and reveals the kind and gentle personality of the goddess and the finest qualities of a loyal and loving wife. She is always at the side of Shiva and holds a lotus in her hand, as well as the mudra offering protection or gifts.

Durga and Kali

▲ Durga. The goddess who is worshipped by those seeking protection, and freedom from illness and difficulties.

Durga and Kali are other forms of Parvati, when the goddess reveals her powers to destroy evil and ignorance.

As Durga, she appears as a brave heroine riding a tiger, showing that she can control this wild and arrogant animal and harness its strength. She carries ferocious weapons in her many arms in order to kill the demon buffalo, which represents ignorance and selfishness.

As Kali, the goddess is shown in her most terrifying form. She has the power of destruction and punishes all evil-doers by killing them. She is dark or black in colour with a red face and her tongue is hanging out to frighten the evil enemies. She wears a garland of skulls around her neck and holds a severed head in her hand. This is strange use of imagery for a goddess but it is intended to show her tremendous power in destroying all forms of evil and ignorance.

Both Kali and Durga, in spite of their frightening appearance, have one hand raised in a special gesture that means, 'Do not fear, I will protect you and goodness will replace evil'.

Lakshmi

▲ Kali. She has devotees who believe in her power to destroy all evil in the world.

▲ Lakshmi. Her worship is connected to hope for prosperity or money.

A New Approach – Hinduism

She is the consort or wife of Vishnu and represents the beauty, prosperity and benevolence of the goddess. She is shown standing or sitting on a lotus with gold coins pouring out of one of her hands and lotus flowers in the others. She wears lots of gold jewellery and a pink sari or pink lotus flowers, as pink is the colour of kindness. She is the goddess of good fortune and Hindus pray to her when they need help with money, and especially at Divali when they hope for a prosperous new year.

Saraswati

She is the consort or wife of Brahma and the goddess of knowledge. This is more than scholarly knowledge but refers to the truths revealed in the scriptures about the nature of God and the inner self. She sits on a lotus and holds sacred scriptures in one hand, mala prayer beads in another, a lotus in another and she also plays the vina or Indian lute with another. This music represents the music of the spheres or cosmos expressed in the syllable Om. So, this aspect of the goddess reminds Hindus of the importance of prayer, studying the scriptures and purity of mind. Her vehicle is the swan, an appropriately graceful, beautiful and pure white bird.

TEST YOURSELF

1 What is the meaning of the word shakti?
2 What kind of powers do goddesses possess?
3 What are the special qualities of Parvati, Durga, Kali, Lakshmi and Saraswati?

TASK BOX

a) Draw pictures of the goddesses and label your pictures, explaining the meaning of the symbols and hand gestures (mudras).
b) Write a paragraph explaining why the goddess is so important in Hinduism.
c) Discuss the following statement: 'It is impossible to think of God in a female form.'

'As a Hindu, I see God in everything, in animals and plants and other human beings. The ultimate being is Brahman, the life force and the Oneness of God. However, Brahman can take any form at all, male, female, animal. So sometimes the gods we worship are male, or female, or both. Sometimes God is show in animal forms, half elephant, like Ganesh, or half monkey, like Hanuman.'

Young Hindu student speaking to the author.

KEY QUESTION

What are the ten avatars of Vishnu?

POPULAR DEITIES

In Hinduism many aspects of God are represented in human and animal form. The most important of these are the ten **avatars** of Vishnu. Avatar is sometimes translated as 'incarnation' or 'living form', but it means more than that. It refers to the ability of God to take any form at all, and the descent of God to planet Earth, where there can be seen to be a decline of goodness and harmony as evil forces influence human actions.

> For whenever the law of righteousness (dharma)
> Withers away, and lawlessness (adharma) raises its head,
> Then do I generate myself on earth.
> For the protection of the good,
> For the destruction of evildoers
> For the setting up of righteousness
> I come into being, age after age.
>
> *Bhagavad Gita, Chapter IV, verses vii–viii* (Zaehner)

The ten principal avatars are:

1 the fish, Matsya
2 the tortoise, Kurma
3 the boar, Varaha
4 the man-lion, Narashinha
5 the dwarf, Vamana
6 Rama (Parasurama), the warrior with the battle axe
7 Rama, the prince
8 Krishna
9 Buddha
10 Kalki.

There are many tales about these avatars in the **Bhagavad Purana**, a collection of stories about the popular gods. These stories about the avatars all contain the same theme of rescuing all living beings, human and animal, from evil and harmful forces.

Some modern scholars think these avatars relate to different stages of evolution as shown here:

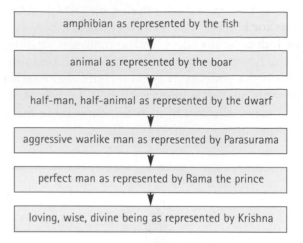

amphibian as represented by the fish
↓
animal as represented by the boar
↓
half-man, half-animal as represented by the dwarf
↓
aggressive warlike man as represented by Parasurama
↓
perfect man as represented by Rama the prince
↓
loving, wise, divine being as represented by Krishna

This shows that there is a deeper meaning to these stories than one might assume at first.

Read the following accounts of the heroic stories about these avatars and see if you can answer the questions at the end of this section.

Matsya the fish rescued Manu, the ancestor of the human race, from a flood.

Kurma the tortoise provided his curved back as a support for a mountain from which the gods and demons churned up the waters of the ocean in order to extract the most important ingredients for life, which had been lost in a flood. This included amrit, the nectar of immortality, Lakshmi the goddess of wealth and beauty, the divine cow, a precious gem, an elephant and a conch shell that would bring victory in battle to anyone who found it.

Narasimha the man-lion came into being when a demon called Hiranyankasipu ruled the Earth. This demon had magical powers so that he could not be killed by any means. The demon did not believe in God, but his son Prahlada did, so the demon tortured his son to stop him believing in God. Narasimha waited until sunset and emerged from a stone pillar at the entrance of the demon's house and killed the demon by tearing him to pieces so Prahlada was free to worship God in peace.

Varaha the boar rescued the Earth using his tusks, after the Earth had been pushed to the bottom of the ocean by a demon.

Vamana the dwarf appeared when another demon controlled the Earth. He approached the demon and asked if he could have all the land he could cover in three steps. Seeing the small size of the dwarf, he agreed. Then Vamana grew to an enormous size and with two paces he covered the Earth and the heavens and with the third step he pressed the demon into the underworld.

Rama the prince came into being when the demon king Ravanna of Sri Lanka ruled the Earth. Rama had been tricked out of becoming king and was exiled to the forest for 14 years with his wife Sita and his brother Lakshamana. While they were living in the forest Sita was kidnapped by Ravanna. With help from the monkey god **Hanuman**, Rama was able to destroy the evil king Ravanna and rescue Sita, and restore peace and happiness to Earth. This story is told at Divali festival.

Parasurama, or Rama with the axe, saved the priests of the faith when they were threatened with destruction by the warriors or Kshatriya. He exterminated 21 generations of the Kshatriya race because of their arrogance and also taught the lesson that a father's command must always be obeyed.

Buddha appeared as a great teacher and taught the doctrine of ahimsa, which means harmlessness and that no creature should be killed. His purpose was to protect the animals.

Krishna is one of the most popular avatars and the stories about him reveal his powers to overcome all kinds of evil and establish goodness and harmony on Earth. His teachings are contained in the **Bhagavad Gita**.

Kalki is the avatar of Vishnu, which is yet to come when evil takes over the world again. It is said that he will come on a white horse carrying a shining sword to destroy evil.

TASK BOX

Discuss the following questions:

a) What are the common themes in all these stories?
b) What are the signs of the decline of goodness and harmony in our present world?
c) Can religion help to restore goodness and harmony to the world today? If not, why not, and if so, how?

Krishna

Krishna is the most popular avatar of Vishnu and is worshipped as a god in his own right. The legends about his life are contained in the Bhagavad Purana and his teachings are found in the Bhagavad Gita, which is part of the Mahabharata (a popular Hindu scripture).

The word Krishna in **Sanskrit** means 'dark'. He is blue in colour to represent the infinity of his divine nature, and clothed in yellow to suggest the earth and so show he is really God in an earthly form.

In the stories about his life it is said that he was born in a jail in the state of Mathura, which was ruled by his cruel tyrant of an uncle, Kamsa, who had taken the throne from his parents. As a baby, Krishna was miraculously rescued and taken to live in Vrindabran ('Cow village') in Gokula, where he was brought up by simple peasant foster parents, Yashoda and Nandi. Krishna's divine nature was revealed through various accounts of his childhood pranks. One day, Yashoda scolded him for swallowing some mud, but when she looked into his open mouth to find the earth, she saw the whole universe and had to worship him as God.

Another story tells of how he overcame a many-headed serpent or dragon, Kaliya, who had been causing the entire village to suffer by polluting the river with poison. In the ensuing battle, Krishna leapt onto the serpent's hood and danced on it, tormenting the serpent so much with his divine weight that the serpent had to ask forgiveness and become a worshipper of Krishna.

This image of Krishna dancing on a serpent's head shows his powers to overcome evil.

Krishna is often shown playing the flute. This represents the enchanting music that brings about the bliss of realising the true nature of God. The milkmaids or **gopis** of Vindabran were enchanted by Krishna's divine music and danced in ecstasy around him. Peacocks also opened their feathers, a symbol of their joy and ecstasy. The gopis remembered him all through the day – whatever they were doing. When he disappeared from view, they would constantly repeat his name, and imitate his gestures and dancing, and sing his praises in many hymns until he reappeared to dance with them. This represents the way in which Krishna's worshippers express their love for him. His favourite gopi was **Radha** and the complete devotion of Krishna for Radha, and Radha for Krishna, represents the never-ending love of God for his devotees and the devotees' complete submission

◀ Krishna playing the flute, with a white calf behind him.

PERSPECTIVES

According to one Hindu writer:

The god Krishna is uniquely Indian. He embodies some of the most attractive things about that ancient civilisation. He is a warrior and dragon-slayer, he has the wisdom of the yogis and the warm heart of a lover.

Nigel Frith, *The Legend of Krishna*, page 9

According to a young Hindu:

'Krishna is my favourite god. He came down to earth to rescue the human race from evil forces. I love Krishna because he is beautiful, full of fun, very lovable and yet very wise. He is very much like us when we play and love our parents and friends.'

Adapted from *Interpreting Religious Hindus*, page 17

to God. Thus Krishna and Radha are often found as the divine couple in Hindu temples and shrines.

This kind of devotion and worship is called **bhakti** and is particularly associated with the worship of Krishna. Vrindavan, on the banks of the Ganges, is a place of pilgrimage for Krishna devotees as it is considered to be the actual place where all his divine exploits took place.

The stories of Krishna's life tell of how he left the village of Vrindaban to reclaim his kingly rights from the evil tryant Kamsa. Through his efforts he destroyed the evil powers and established peace and order in the land of Mathura. Thus Krishna is shown wearing a crown to depict his qualities as a good monarch guarding the welfare of all beings. Of all the Hindu gods, Krishna is the one best known in the West.

The Krishna Consciousness movement is well established in Britain. This movement originated in India in the sixteenth century BCE through the teachings of the Hindu saint Caitanya. He emphasised the path of bhakti yoga, which is complete loving devotion and submission to Lord Krishna as the ultimate god. This form of Hinduism was started in the West in the 1960s by Swami Prabupada, who in his later years travelled to America to teach the message of Lord Krishna for the first time to people in the West. This has become an international movement now, known as ISKCON (International Society for Krishna Consciousness). These Hindus live a life based on the principles of the brahmacharya stage in life, developing a pure body and mind through regular prayer, chanting and meditation. They practise bhakti yoga through their chanting and devotional worship and are a familiar sight in Britain's main cities. They have become widely known for their charity work and for offering free food to the poor and homeless.

▲ Western Hindus in London.

PERSPECTIVES

Boy George had a top ten song devoted to Krishna and former Beatle George Harrison was also a devotee. The International Society for Krishna Consciousness (ISKCON) started in America in the 1960s, but had its origin in India in the sixteenth century. This movement opened up Hinduism to Westerners. Its members are devoted to Lord Krishna and are often seen in Western cities singing their famous 'Hare Krishna' chant. They encourage pure living and vegetarianism and have set up special cafés offering free food to those in need.

TEST YOURSELF

1 Why is Krishna such a popular Indian deity?
2 What is the meaning of these symbols, which are often associated with Krishna: blue skin, yellow garments, a peacock feather, a bejewelled crown, a flute and a white calf?
3 What is meant by bhakti?
4 How might devotees of Krishna show their devotion to him?

Rama

Rama is another very popular avatar of Vishnu. He is considered to be one of the most glorious of all the characters in the Ramayana. This is the epic in which most of the stories about Rama are found. In his earthly form he was born as the eldest son of King Dasaratha and he was renowned for his excellent skill in archery. His bow and arrow are his weapons to fight against evil. He carries them at all times to show his readiness and alertness to fight against injustice, inequality and establish peace and justice. In the stories about the life of Rama, he is the ideal human being, providing a role model as a perfect son, an ideal king, a true husband, a real friend and a noble enemy. His wife is Sita and she too represents the qualities of loyalty, caring and devotion that the ideal wife should have.

The Ramayana gives an account of a famous story of Rama, which is celebrated at the festival of Divali.

On the eve of Rama's coronation in the city of Ayodhya, his step-mother Kaikeyi demanded that her son Bharat be crowned and that Rama be sent to the forest for 14 years. Rama knew that his father, the ageing king Dasaratha, would not survive the sorrow and so he left. Rama would not compromise with the fulfilment of duty.

While Rama, his wife Sita, and his brother Lakshmana were exiled in the forest, the demon king of Sri Lanka, Ravanna, kidnapped Sita and took her away to his Sri Lankan kingdom. Rama made enormous efforts to find her, and then, with the help of Hanuman, king of the monkeys, and all the animals of the forest, he attempted to rescue her. After many heroic events, including building an enormous bridge to Lanka, the evil king Ravanna was overcome and Sita was rescued. So they both returned to establish a peaceful and prosperous kingdom in Ayodhya.

Sita is a popular deity with some Hindus because of her qualities of courage, faithfulness and her ability to bring an abundance of wealth to the home and the kingdom.

The evil king Ravanna is often shown with ten heads (see opposite). These symbolise the knowledge that he had acquired, but which he used for harm rather than good. He had become proud and arrogant. In defeating Ravanna, Rama's victory can be seen as the triumph of goodness and kindness in human nature over anger and pride. So the story can be understood in a variety of ways, as a wonderful mythical tale in which goodness triumphs over evil, or as the battle within the human personality to become a better person and acknowledge the reality of God within each living being and the whole of the universe.

◀ **Rama with Hanuman and attendants.**

▲ Ravanna, the demon king of Sri Lanka.

Ganesha

At first, the image of this god is very puzzling, but when one finds out the meaning of the symbols and the stories that explain them, it is possible to appreciate why this god is so important to Hindus.

The name **Ganesha** in Sanskrit means 'multitude', and 'Isa' means Lord, so his name means 'Lord of all Beings'. Since Ganesha is the first son of Lord Shiva this is an appropriate title for him. He is also known as Ganapati and Gajanana. 'Gaja' means 'elephant', 'anana' means 'face', so Gajanana means 'elephant-faced'.

Ganesha is the god of obstacles and people pray to him to remove obstacles from their lives. His statue is found at city gates, or guarding temple doorways and house doors, as he represents the doorkeeper of the universe.

There is a story of how Ganesha received his elephant head, which is that he was moulded from clay by Parvati to guard her bathroom door. Her husband, Shiva, came to her one night but the door was being guarded by Ganesha, who did not allow him to go into Parvati's room. Shiva was so angry at being refused access that he cut off Ganesha's head. However, Parvati was so distressed that, in remorse, Shiva replaced it with the head of an elephant.

In another version of the story, Parvati made an image of a child with an elephant's head and threw it into the river Ganges where it was brought to life.

In another story, Ganesha is said to have lost his trunk in a fight. Therefore, in many statues he is shown holding it in his hand like a pen. The pen represents scholarship and wisdom, so Ganesha is considered to be the author of the sacred Vedic scriptures.

Ganesha is usually pictured as having a human form with an elephant head, and with one tusk broken. He has a conspicuously large stomach and sits with one leg folded in, and at his feet a variety of food is laid out. A rat sits near the food and looks up at him as if asking permission to eat the food. All these symbols represent the ways to reach the state of human perfection and become one with God.

▲ A painting of Ganesha. Notice his raised hand with the swastika symbol.

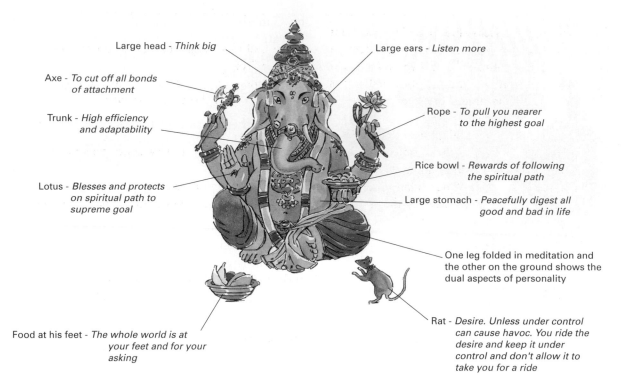

Large head - *Think big*

Large ears - *Listen more*

Axe - *To cut off all bonds of attachment*

Rope - *To pull you nearer to the highest goal*

Trunk - *High efficiency and adaptability*

Rice bowl - *Rewards of following the spiritual path*

Lotus - *Blesses and protects on spiritual path to supreme goal*

Large stomach - *Peacefully digest all good and bad in life*

One leg folded in meditation and the other on the ground shows the dual aspects of personality

Food at his feet - *The whole world is at your feet and for your asking*

Rat - *Desire. Unless under control can cause havoc. You ride the desire and keep it under control and don't allow it to take you for a ride*

His large ears and head indicate his great wisdom, which has been acquired by listening carefully to the eternal truths of the Vedic scriptures.

The elephant's trunk is like a very special tool as the elephant can pick up trees with it, as well as tiny objects from the ground. So, it is a symbol of the intellect that can discriminate and distinguish between truth and falsehood.

The large stomach suggests that Ganesha can 'digest' whatever happens to him, no matter how difficult, so that he is not overcome with the losses, suffering and grief of life, or carried away with his successes and achievements.

One leg folded and the other on the ground shows the two aspects of his personality in balance. One side is firmly rooted in worldly things and the other is engaged in meditation and concentration on God and the inner spiritual self, called the atman.

The food at his feet denotes the wealth, power and prosperity that he has at his command but which do not rule his life.

The rat represents greed and desire, as the rat hoards more than it needs to and steals from others. The rat looks for guidance from Ganesha to overcome these greedy desires in order to find the spiritual path to perfection. The rat is Ganesha's vehicle showing that the overcoming of desires provides enough strength to even transport an elephant.

In each of his four arms Ganesha holds objects that symbolise the path to God. The axe represents the destruction of selfish desires, the rope is a means to pull the person away from worldly attachments, the rice bowl shows the rewards of spiritual seeking, and the lotus is a symbol of the purity of the mind in a person who has reached the final goal.

TEST YOURSELF

A B C

1 What are the special qualities of Krishna, Rama and Ganesha?

2 Why might a Hindu choose to worship each of these?

TASK BOX

Discuss the following questions.

a) Hindus have no difficulty in believing that God might take a human or animal form. What do you think about this possibility?

b) A Hindu might worship their favourite personal god as well as meditating on the nature of the Supreme Being – Brahman – and discover God within themselves.

  (i)   What is meant by 'a personal god'?
  (ii) Why might some Hindus find it easier to worship a personal god rather than meditating on Brahman?
  (iii) What is the difference between worship and meditation?

c) 'It is extremely difficult to understand the Hindu concept of God unless you are a Hindu yourself.'

---

1 a) What are the functions of Brahma, Vishnu and Shiva in the Hindu trimurti of God? (3 marks)

  b) **Either**

    (i) Choose one these gods and explain the meaning of the symbols associated with them.

    Or

    (ii) Look at the picture of Shiva on page 29 and read the text. Explain the meaning of seven symbols associated with Shiva. (7 marks)

  c) What effect might a belief in these gods have on a Hindu's attitude to:

    (i)   the way they behave in this life?
    (ii) the universe around them?
    (iii) their purpose in this life? (6 marks)

  d) Do you think that Hindus believe in one God or in many gods?

  Give reasons for your answer. (5 marks)

2 a) Krishna and Rama are avatars of the god Vishnu. What is meant by the term 'avatar'? (3 marks)

  b) Choose **either** Krishna **or** Rama.

    (i)   Give an account of a story associated with them. (4 marks)

    (ii) Name three symbols that would enable you to recognise this deity. (3 marks)

    (iii) Explain their special powers through the stories and symbols associated with them. (5 marks)

    (iv) How might a devotion to this deity affect a Hindu's behaviour in everyday life ? (4 marks)

  c) 'Krishna is the most popular deity in Hinduism.'

  Do you agree or disagree with this view? Give reasons for your answer showing you have considered more than one point of view. (5 marks)

Assignment

REMEMBER

- Hindus believe there is one God that has many forms.
- Brahman means the life-giving power within the universe.
- Om is the sound made by Brahman.
- The Hindu trimurti is: Brahma (creator), Vishnu (preserver), Shiva (destroyer and re-creator).
- Shakti refers to the goddess as the creative energy that is used to breathe life into the world. Shakti takes many different forms: Parvati, Durga, Kali, Lakshmi, Saraswati.
- The avatars of Vishnu are the representations of Vishnu in human and animal form.
- Krishna is an important avatar of Vishnu and is worshipped as a god.
- Rama is another popular avatar of Vishnu and a famous story about him is celebrated at Divali.
- Ganesha is the god who removes obstacles.

WEBLINKS

- http://www.hindunet.org/god/Gods/brahma/index.htm
- http://www.goloka.com/index.html
  Find pictures of the incarnations of Vishnu.
- http://www.indiaoz.com.au/hinduism/pictures/index.shtml.
  Find some lovely pictures of the Hindu gods and identify the main symbols and their meaning. Also look on this site to find out about the Om symbol.
- http://cleo.net.uk/display2.cfm?subject=11&group=1&module=content%2Fre%2Ftemplel
  The website of Cumbria Education on-line will take you on a multi-media exploration of a Hindu temple in Preston. Explore the pages on 'God, Gods and Goddesses', and 'The Gallery' to view more images of the deities.
- http://www.hinduism.fsnet.co.uk/schools1s2.htm
  Go to 'index and fact finder' and look up 'Gods without form'.
- http://www.isckon.com
  Find out about the history and beliefs of the International Society for Krishna Consciousness, their membership and work around the world.

UNIT THREE | Worship

3

KEY WORDS

Arti: offerings of light to the deity.

Bhajan: special song and hymn to god.

Bhakti: loving devotion to the deity.

Darshan: viewing with respect a holy image and receiving a divine blessing in return.

Deity: one of the many forms of Brahman in the form of a particular god.

Devotee: one who is devoted to a god.

Garbha-griha: the inner shrine or womb house, containing the image of the deity.

Gayatri mantra: a famous Hindu prayer usually chanted at puja.

Gopuram: large towers or gateways found in temples in southern India.

Kirtan: devotional singing.

Mandapa: the pillared hallway or passageway leading to the inner shrine.

Murti: the image of the deity that has been installed in the shrine.

Prashad: food that has been offered to the gods and then given out to the worshippers.

Puja: worship or paying respects to God or a chosen deity.

Sandalwood: sweet-smelling oil or incense used in puja.

Shikhara: a tower or spire above the image of the deity inside the temple.

Shrine: a place set aside for puja with images of the deity, flowers, lights and incense.

Yajna: a ritual that involves a form of sacrifice.

KEY QUESTION

How do Hindus relate to God?

Worship is a way of expressing faith and relating to God. This is shown through special actions or rituals. Many Hindus relate to God through the many different forms and images of the popular **deities** and saints. In response to the question, 'Why do Hindus worship images and idols?', a Hindu priest explained to his questioner:

PERSPECTIVES

'A believer sees in an image or idol what a non-believer cannot see. The immense faith and devotion that a person pours into an idol turns that idol into God for him. Perhaps it is only a stone to others but to him it is God. We believe that God is omnipresent, that is, He is everywhere. If He is everywhere then surely He is in that idol too. Also the great sages of India knew that ordinary people would find it difficult to concentrate, so the image is used as a point of concentration to focus their minds, and to meditate and communicate with God. So when we pray with the image in front of us, this makes us aware of God's presence and we feel he is with us and we are able to ask him to bless us with the good things in life.'

The chosen deity is regarded as an honoured guest in the home and is treated like royalty in the magnificent temples and **shrines**. Throughout India, in every possible place – shops, cafés, taxis, lorry cabs, roundabouts, inside banyan trees – shrines of the deities are found. Many Hindus worship these deities at the shrines, or in temples, and especially in the home.

PUJA

Puja is the nearest word in Hinduism to the word 'worship'. It actually means paying respects or homage to God through various actions that express the wish to please the chosen deity and offer service to them and hope for the blessing of God in return. The same basic rituals of puja are performed at the shrine in the home as well as in the temple – one being simple, the other more elaborate and dramatic. It is an individual act of devotion and each person performs it in their own way.

◀ **Images on the tower of the temple of Kumbhewara.**

▲ Worship can take many forms, from elaborate rituals to a simple act of devotion or showing of respect to a holy place, image or person.

PUJA IN THE HOME

In every Hindu home there will be a place set aside for a small shrine to their chosen and favourite family deity, usually in a small room or a specially fitted cupboard or shelf. Puja is generally performed by women, although it can involve all family members, and takes place every day in the morning and evening.

Objects found on a shrine in the home

These would include images and pictures of the gods and goddesses. The items used in puja usually include:

- a small (usually copper) vessel containing water from the holy river Ganges
- red kum-kum powder, yellow turmeric powder, **sandalwood** paste
- flowers and leaves
- food offering of sweetmeats and fresh fruit
- incense

- a small ghee lamp (usually a small dish with a cotton wool wick placed in ghee or clarified butter)
- an **arti** lamp
- a small bell.

Now look at the photograph below of the shrine set up in a home and pick out these items in it.

The actions of puja and their meaning

Every day the deity is 'awakened' and treated in the same way as an honoured guest would be treated.

1 Before puja in the home, those participating will bathe and dress in clean clothes. This shows respect and the desire to clean not just the body but also the soul, and to clear away ignorance.
2 The deity is invited to be present in the image by special prayers and ringing of the bell.

▲ Puja in the home. On this shrine you can see items used for puja. Notice the various images and pictures of deities and one or two members of the family who have died.

▲ Shrines are made to fit anywhere. This one is on the typical steps (or ghats) that are found alongside the river Ganges. The shrine has been made to fit into the architecture.

3 The deity is offered a special seat and welcomed like an honoured guest, and a water offering is made in a similar way.

4 The deities are given a ceremonial bath using panchamrit, a mixture of milk, yoghurt, sugar, honey and butter. The image is washed with clean water and dried. It is given fresh clothes specially made to fit the image. Sometimes, a sacred thread is placed on it.

5 Next turmeric powder, red kum-kum powder and sandalwood paste is put on each deity and rice is placed in front of it. Sandalwood is known to have a calming effect and this action enables the worshipper to remove any anxiety and feel calm and relaxed.

▲ This is a shrine to Krishna. He is shown playing a flute and with his consort Radha.

A New Approach – Hinduism

6   Brightly coloured, sweet-smelling flowers are laid before the figures or hung over them as garlands. The offering of the flowers should be done in a particular way. The five fingers of the right hand are used to pick up the flower gently, then the fingers are turned upwards with the flower, which is softly offered at the deity's feet. The flowers represent worldly desires and the offering of flowers shows the willingness to get rid of one's desires and express love and devotion for the deity.

7   Incense sticks are lit to create a fragrant atmosphere and perfumed oils are burnt to represent the destruction of selfish desires, and in order to create a pleasing atmosphere.

8   Then a small ghee lamp is lit and waved before the deity.

9   Fruits and food, usually rice in India, are ceremonially offered to the deity to thank God for the bounty given by him to all beings. Coconut and betel leaves might be arranged around the deity.

10 The arti ceremony is then performed. A special arti dish containing five cotton wool wicks dipped in purified butter is lit. The number five represents the five elements of earth, air, wind, water and fire. This lamp is rotated around the deity while a small bell is rung. Then the **devotees** symbolically accept the light and blessing of God by passing their hands over the flame and then placing the palms of their hands over their eyes, forehead and head. This action represents the wish to destroy the darkness of ignorance and receive the light of knowledge.

11 Some of the food offered to the deity is then distributed and eaten by those present as **prashad**, or blessed food.

The purpose of puja

All of the items used in puja relate to the five elements of earth, air, fire, wind and water, and the five senses of sight, hearing, touch, taste and smell. These are the basic ingredients of life and show how, in the act of puja, the basic elements of life are offered to God and express gratitude for the gift of life. So, all the actions of puja are performed for the specific purpose of bringing the presence of the deity into the home and to help the worshipper develop a good state of mind, with loving feelings towards God and all beings. It also helps to concentrate on the inner self in order to seek wisdom and understanding.

TEST YOURSELF

A B C

1   What is puja?
2   What objects are used in puja?
3   What actions are performed in puja?

TASK BOX

Look at the picture on pages 46–8, or use pictures or video clips on the websites listed at the end of this chapter, of Hindus performing puja in the home or at a shrine.

a) Identify the main actions and write down the meaning and purpose of these actions.
b) How might offering daily puja affect a Hindu's attitude to the day ahead and the rest of their daily life?
c) Discuss why you think some religious people like to worship God in their home, while others prefer to go to a special place for worship like a temple or church.

Prayers during puja

Two important prayers or mantras are recited during puja. One is the arti prayer:

> O Lord of the universe, Supreme Soul, Dispeller of sorrow, hail to you. Your rule of righteousness be established everywhere, it is you who banishes in an instant the troubles of your devotees. May your kingdom of virtue reign supreme. Whoever meditates upon you receives your grace. The worries of his mind disappear: his home is blessed with peace, happiness and plenty and all his bodily pains vanish …
> Destroy our base desires and wipe out our sins, increase our faith and devotion. May we serve you and your devotees.

The other is the **Gayatri mantra**:

> Om Bhur swah. Tatsavitur varenyam bhargo devasya dhimahi, dhio yo nah prachodayat.
> The Protector, Who is the basis of life of the whole universe and who is self existent.
> Who is free from all pains and Whose contact frees the souls from all troubles
> pervades this multi-formed universe and sustains all.
> He is the Creator and Energiser of the whole universe, the Giver of all happiness,
> Worthy of acceptance, the most Excellent.
> Pure and Purifier.
> That very God. Let us embrace so that God may direct our minds.

OTHER FORMS OF WORSHIP

Bhakti

Bhakti is a deep, intense and personal devotion to the god Bhakti and is sometimes expressed in devotional worship of a congregational kind, for instance, **kirtan**. Devotees gather in groups and sing **bhajans** (hymns) written by famous poets and saints.

Havan

This is a fire sacrifice that is performed on special occasions, usually at the temple. The fire is the god Agni (an ancient Vedic God) and offerings of rice and ghee are offered to this fire.

Yajna

Yajna is a form of public worship in which the community gathers to worship God and express their intention to be selfless and dedicated in their service to the community. It is a kind of sacrifice and is based on the same ideas of the ancient Vedic rituals of the Brahmin priests. Today, it expresses the giving-up or sacrifice of personal desires and self-centredness.

Trees being worshipped by women pilgrims during Karttik (Karttik is the name of the month that runs from mid-October to mid-November). They are tying galtas around a sacred tree. Many trees are considered sacred in India, especially banyan and pipal trees.

Yoga

Most people in the West think yoga is a special form of exercise involving various postures and some meditation for general well-being and health, but yoga is much more than this within Hinduism. Just as puja and other forms of worship are ways of relating to and uniting with God, so yoga is a means of bringing union with a personal god or the supreme being, Brahman. However, yoga requires strong commitment and great self-discipline.

There are at least four ways of doing this: karma yoga, bhakti yoga, jnana yoga and raja yoga.

Karma yoga is the path of unselfish action by doing the daily work and particular duties of your stage in life and caste, without a desire for reward or selfish gain. Talent and fulfilling your own potential for the good of society is considered to be the path of karma yoga. Gandhi, who worked tirelessly and selflessly in campaigns for Indian independence and the upliftment of the untouchables, was seen as the ideal karma yogi.

Bhakti yoga is the path of devotion to God. This is expressed in a loving relationship with a personal deity in which the devotee remembers the god's name constantly and praises him or her through singing and chanting. The devotee surrenders to their chosen lord completely and with great emotion experiences the peace and love of God. This enables them to take refuge in God and eventually reach moksha.

Jnana yoga is the path of knowledge and understanding. This path is achieved through deep meditation and an experience of oneness with the supreme spirit Brahman. This path enables you to see how temporary life is and how you can gain true wisdom, knowledge and happiness.

Raja yoga or 'royal yoga' is regarded by some Hindus as the highest form of yoga and the fulfilment of all of the other three ways. This is a form of self-control over both the senses and the mind. It involves deep contemplation of Brahman and, when success is achieved, the personality is transformed and freed from anger, lust, greed, envy and sadness.

The mandir: Hindu temples and shrines in India

Key Question
What are Hindu temples and shrines like?

India is sometimes called the land of temples as they are situated in places associated with appearances of the gods or where special miracles may have taken place. Shrines are like miniature temples and are found in many different forms in every village and along the roadside. The mandir is often the most prominent building in the village and is made of brick, which is brightly painted and decorated with images of the gods. In small towns, especially those alongside a river, the temple would be placed near to the edge of the river with steps reaching down into the water.

Some temples are important centres of learning and research, while others specialise in providing help to the needy through charitable works, medical care and support. They are important at festival times when the elaborate public processions are organised from them and everyone from the local community is involved.

The Hindu temple or mandir is a symbol with many meanings. It is intended to be a special place for the encounter between the worshipper and the divine, a place where the divine and human can meet. Many temples are associated with places where the gods may have appeared. They are not meeting places for a congregation, but for the individual worshipper or small group. The idea is to leave the busy world behind as you go through the gateway to approach the inner shrine and to seek the truth within you. Just as with any religious building, it is designed to help produce a certain state of mind. The external surroundings remind the worshipper of the special nature and qualities of their god. It is a way of creating a kind of divine realm or a kind of heaven on earth.

The Hindu temple is a symbol of the universe, and the different designs and plans correspond to the regions of the earth and sky and the homes of the various gods.

▲ The Sri Siva Subramaniya temple in Fiji. Notice the style of the temple, which is also an example of how Hinduism has spread beyond India.

The design of Hindu temples

In Hindu mythology, mountains are the dwelling places of the gods so, in the Himalayas, Kailasha, also called Mount Meru, is both the centre of the world and the home of Shiva and Parvati. Therefore, the basic shape of a temple is meant to be like a mountain and to provide the most beautiful and splendid palace for the gods who are like divine royalty dwelling in their mansions on earth. There is a difference of style in the shape and layout of temples in the north and south of India, but there are some basic features that all temples have.

The basic purpose of the mandir is to house the deities, so the centre and focus of the whole building is the inner sanctum where the image or **murti** of the deity is installed. This room or place is called the **garbha-griha**, which means 'womb house', and directly above this is the **shikhara**, a tower-like structure or spire, which is placed above the image of the deities in the innermost chamber of the temple. It also represents the highest level of the mind or liberation (moksha) and the tower leads the eye upwards towards liberation.

▲ The Meenakshi temple in Madurai, India.

The space in front of the shrine is often a pillared hallway called a **mandapa**. Some temples have a covered porch or entrance hall with steps leading up to the mandapa. At the entrance to the temple there is sometimes a separate shrine that houses the guardian of the deity and is usually the vehicle of the deity, for example, Nandi the bull for Shiva and Garuda the eagle for Vishnu. In large temples there are other shrines to the consorts of the deities around the mandapa or front entrance hall. Many temples have a circular path around the inner sanctum so that the worshippers can circumambulate (walk around) the deity.

The outside of the temple may have many elaborate decorations showing the stories and legends of the gods and events from the great epics such as the Mahabharata.

The style of temple in the south of India is different. Their most prominent feature is not the shikhara but the **gopuram**, which are towers or large gateways in the outer walls. Some of these gopurams are very famous for their elaborate and decorative sculptures, such as the Meenakshi temple at Madurai.

A New Approach – Hinduism

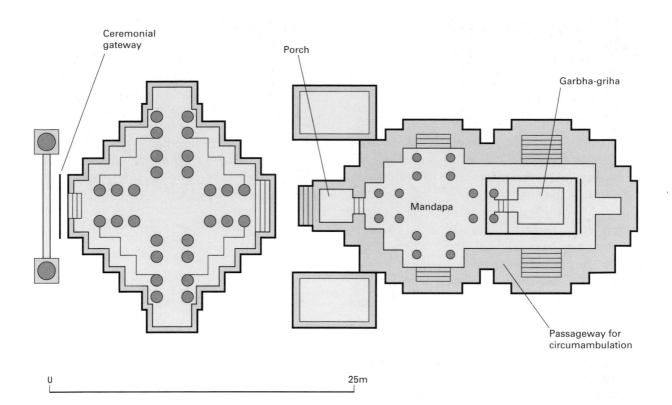

Ceremonial gateway

Porch

Garbha-griha

Mandapa

Passageway for circumambulation

0   25m

▲ A plan of a traditional Hindu temple.

▲ Hindus bathe in a pool before entering a Bhubaneshwar temple. The complex consists of a towered sanctuary, a square mandapa with a pyramidal roof, an architrave gateway and a large bathing tank. Visitors must be clean before entering the inner sanctum.

▲ This shows the elaborate Shikhara of a famous Shaivite temple in Bombay.

The rituals that take place as part of the daily life in the temple revolve around the daily needs of the deities, and so they are dressed, bathed and garlanded, given food offerings and put to rest.

When Hindus visit a temple it will be for a special purpose or intention or a festival occasion. They will perform their own individual puja or join in congregational worship. The worshipper has to be in a state of ritual purity in order to receive the divine blessings. Menstruating women and some of the lower castes are often barred from entering temples. Men and women wear traditional dress rather than Western clothes.

They will remove their shoes on entering and ring the bell near the entrance and then perform some or all of the following ritual actions.

The purpose of temple worship helps the worshipper to withdraw from the outside world and look into the inner self and the divine nature within, and become fully aware of the presence of God in their lives. They can then return to the world spiritually refreshed.

◄ Prostration before the chosen deity. For this ritual the devotee lies flat on their stomach with their arms stretched over their head, with palms together in a gesture of humility and desire to serve God. This Hindu pilgrim prepares to prostrate himself before a temple of Krishna.

▲ Circumambulation of the temple. This is walking around the temple or the inner walkway three times, with the temple on the right side, a traditional sign of respect.

▲ Offerings of flowers and fruit. The coconut is often offered as it is a symbol of the pure inner self within a tough outer shell. This might be given to the temple priest who will break the shell and tear the tuft and pour the pure milk over the murti.

▲ Arti. Arti might be performed as well as other acts of puja, along with quiet meditation or reading of sacred scriptures.

◀ **Darshan**. The most important part of the temple worship is darshan, which is the viewing of the image in the inner shrine. The garbha-griha is dark like a cave in a mountain and the priest reveals the image by the light of the flame in the tray. The worshipper passes their right hand over the flame and makes offerings of flowers and fruit and a donation to the priest. Then the worshipper is given a flower or garland from the shrine as a token of the god's grace. In some temples, worshippers are given some prashad to eat.

HINDU TEMPLES IN BRITAIN

▲ In Britain, the Hindu community have put a great deal of effort and commitment into creating new mandirs. At first they converted existing buildings, but have more recently created purpose-built temples. A famous example of these is Swami Narayan temple in Neasden, London.

Look at the website for the Swami Narayan mandir in Neasden (see page 59) and find out how and why it was built.

There are approximately one million Hindus living in Britain today, most of whom have come from the Punjab or Gujarat (regions in India) and the Asian community in East Africa. There are now quite sizeable Hindu communities in most of the major cities and during the last ten years there have been several new temples built and existing ones improved. Most Hindu temples in Britain have been converted from existing houses or church halls, but recently there have been some purpose-built ones. The most notable is the Swami Narayan temple in Neasden, London, for which special craftsmen were brought from India to construct a most beautiful temple in the finest marble.

These temples are very important for the Hindu community in Britain as they serve a social, cultural and religious purpose. They provide a focus for the community to meet and strengthen social and cultural bonds as a minority community in a Western culture.

Since many British Hindus are not able to perform elaborate puja at home, the temple is especially important for preserving religious traditions and instructing the younger generations in the Hindu culture. In Britain, there is much more emphasis on congregational worship than in India. Hindus will travel some distance to attend these services as it gives them a valuable chance to meet up with other Hindu families, as well as engage in worship.

Most Hindu mandirs in Britain have developed a community centre alongside the temple, in which a variety of activities take place.

▲ Hindu boys in a scripture lesson in a temple in the UK.

These include:

- language classes in Gujarati
- cultural activities and classes in music and Indian dance
- youth clubs
- senior citizens' luncheon clubs
- special talks and lectures from visiting holy men (swamis)
- weddings.

As the Hindu community becomes more established, they improve and develop their temples and are able to pay for the full-time services of temple priests. This means they are able to maintain and preserve their cultural traditions, their social bonds with other Hindus and their religious rituals by having their own temples in Britain.

TASK

Using pictures of Hindu temples in this chapter or images on websites listed at the end of this chapter:
(i) identify and label the main features
(ii) explain the purpose of each feature.

REMEMBER

▶ Puja is worshipping a chosen god and can be performed in the temple or at home.
▶ The four forms of yoga are: bhakti, karma, jnana and raja.
▶ The design of Hindu temples can include: murtis, garbha-griha, shikhara and gopuram.
▶ Worship in the temples is called darshan and prashad.

TEST YOURSELF

1 What is the difference between a shrine and a temple?
2 What are the following: shikhara, garbha-griha, mandapa, murti, darshan, gopuram?

1 a) What are the main features of Hindu temples in India?   (8 marks)

  b) Explain why large temples are important in Hinduism.   (6 marks)

  c) 'Hindu temples have a completely different function in India than in Britain.'

  Do you agree or disagree with this view? Give reasons for your answer with reference to another point of view.   (8 marks)

2 a) What are the main actions performed during puja and what is their meaning?   (8 marks)

  b) Why do Hindus perform daily puja in their homes?   (6 marks)

  c) What is the religious meaning of the arti ceremony?   (4 marks)

  d) 'Hinduism is a religion of the home rather than the temple.'

  Do you agree with this view? Give reasons for your answer showing you have considered more than one point of view.   (6 marks)

Assignment

🕸 http://www.bbc.co.uk/
religion/religions/hinduism/
worship/index.shtml
Revise worship.

🕸 http://www.cleo.net.uk/
display2.cfm?subject=11&
group=1&module=content/
re/templet
*Discover a virtual tour of a Hindu
temple. Look up the worship section too.*

🕸 http://www.archaka.com/
Discover more about Hindu puja.

🕸 http://www.hinduism.fsnet.co.uk/
schools1p4.htm
*Find the Hindu prayers, especially the
gayatri mantra.*

🕸 http://www.hinduism.fsnet.co.uk/
schools1s6.htm
*Read and enjoy some Hindu stories.
Look up some passages from the
scriptures. Find out more about worship.*

🕸 http://www.indiantemples.com
🕸 http://www.mandirnet.org/
temple_photos
🕸 http://www.templenet.com/
*Look at lots of pictures of Hindu temples
and find out about their main features
and what happens inside them.*

🕸 http://www.mandir.org/
*Find out all about the Swami Narayan
temple in London.*

WEBLINKS

UNIT FOUR | Festivals

4

KEY WORDS

Ayodhya: the city belonging to Rama referred to in the Divali story.

Divali: festival of lights.

Durga Puja and Dusserah: a ten-day festival in the month of Ahwin celebrating various events from the Hindu epics, the Ramayana and Mahabharata, but especially a goddess festival lasting for ten days.

Holi: the spring festival.

Navaratri: festival for the goddess lasting nine days.

Rakhi: friendship band.

Raksha Bandan: a festival celebrating family bonds and friendship through tying a special friendship band or bracelet around a brother's wrist.

Rangoli: special patterns made with coloured chalks and powders drawn on the floor.

Ratha-yatra: a large procession that takes place at festival times.

Ravanna: demon king.

KEY QUESTION

Why are festivals an important feature of the Hindu way of life?

Festivals are celebrated in every culture in the world. Some festivals happen at key points in the year, for example, the beginnings and endings of each year and the seasons; others are to express the feelings of hope and fulfilment. There are religious festivals based on religious teachings or special events, which provide the opportunity to express religious devotion and renew commitment to the faith. They are times when families and communities gather together to enjoy each other's company and celebrate the values and beliefs they hold in common. They link a community with the past by remembering important historical and religious events that have influenced the present situation.

RATHA-YATRA

Hinduism has a variety of festivals, some clearly related to seasonal changes, others to particular deities. In India, some festivals are marked by splendid public chariot processions called **ratha-yatra**, which begin at the temple and proceed through the streets with specially laden carts and lorries. The lorries are highly decorated and contain images of the deities, which are taken on parade throughout the village, town or city, together with elephants in regalia, street music, dancing and singing. The images of the deities are made from clay, wood or cow dung, and are dressed in ceremonial robes, garlands and crowns. The temple murtis are consecrated and should not be used for this purpose. The procession passes by devotees' dwelling places so they can offer puja as it passes by. A famous procession takes place from the Jagannath temple at Puri and the special chariot for the deity is so large that the word juggernaut originated from this event. At the end of the festival the images of the deities are ceremoniously thrown into the nearest river.

HOLI

Holi is a seasonal festival that celebrates the coming of spring with the joys and hope for a year of abundance in nature and happiness in family relationships and friendships. It is one of the most joyful festivals and is a time for fun as much as religious devotion. It is celebrated on the full moon of the Hindu month of Phalguna, which can be in February or March, and at the start of India's dry season.

◀ The procession of chariots from the Sri Jagannath temple in Puri, India, during the Ratha-yatra festival.

The procession of Maharumbhasan ▶ Tanthavur from the temple. This is the part of the festival when people engage in cleaning the murtis and sculptures of the deities. A coconut is garlanded and held aloft by the worshippers. The coconut is used as a symbol of the pure self inside the coarse outer body, and they are therefore often used as offerings to the deities.

▲ These people are celebrating at a festival of Holi in a temple.

▲ A family celebrates Holi together in Vrindavan.

A New Approach – Hinduism

What do Hindus do at Holi?

There is a custom of lighting a bonfire on the eve of Holi and of roasting grains of popcorn, chick-peas and coconut in the fire as offerings to the gods. These are later shared out as prashad. These roasted grains are called Holuk, giving Holi its name, as well as the story of Holika, which is linked with this festival. When the fire is blazing, people walk around it carrying their children and babies and making offerings of grains to the fire.

It is known as the festival of colour because it is celebrated with coloured powders and water, which everyone throws at each other with lots of fun and laughter. This is a festival in which one is allowed to break some of the usual rules of behaviour so there is a lot of teasing as people wear their old clothes. All barriers of caste and rank are forgotten as people throw coloured water and bright powders at each other. Students chase their teachers down the streets and workers spray their bosses. In the afternoon, people go home for a bath, visit family and friends, and exchange sweets and good wishes among themselves.

In Britain, it is not possible to have a public holiday and such exuberant celebrations in the streets, but Hindus do gather at their community centre or sometimes at a nearby park and have a bonfire and party.

▲ This is an effigy of Holika that has been placed on the ghats near the river Ganges. Later, it will be burnt in a bonfire for Holi celebrations to symbolise the destruction of evil forces and the triumph of goodness.

Stories told at Holi express the theme of goodness overcoming evil. The most significant of these is the one about Holika and Prahlad.

Holika and Prahlad

There was a tyrant of a king called Hiranyakashipu who demanded that everyone should worship him as he considered himself to be the lord of the universe, but his son Prahlad would only worship Vishnu. The king tried to force his son to bow down to him, but Prahlad resisted. The king set out to kill him and persuaded his sister Holika to carry Prahlad into the flames of a furnace. She had been promised by her evil brother that she had a gift from the gods that would save her from being burnt. But this promise did not work and she was burned in the flames. Her brother, who was loyal to god, was miraculously saved.

This story reminds Hindus of the rewards of loyalty and devotion to God and how this faith can overcome evil. Other Holi stories focus on Krishna as a young cowherd who enchanted the milk-maids with the music of his flute. Songs and dances tell of the love between Krishna and his lover, Radha.

The total self-surrender of Radha to her lord reminds Hindus of the need to surrender themselves in devotion to God.

The meaning of Holi

The significance of the colours used at Holi are to express delight at the beauty of the created world. So, the religious meaning of this festival is to express the happiness of being alive and to remove the barriers of hatred and bitterness that cause unhappiness between people. It is also to remind Hindus of the importance of loyalty and devotion to God and the belief that goodness can overcome evil.

The social meaning is to celebrate togetherness and unite in friendship with all people, regardless of caste and social background. This festival helps to renew bonds of friendship and unity among families and the community.

RAKSHA BANDAN

This is celebrated on the day of the full moon in the month of Shravan (August). It is especially popular among British Hindus as it provides a chance to strengthen family bonds with families in India. It is celebrated in the home and all women, both young and old, rise early and, before eating, tie a silk thread with a bright shiny decoration on it around the right wrist of each of their brothers. They then give their brothers some sweet meats. Occasionally, the girls receive a sari in return. The thread is called a raksha or a **rakhi**, which means 'protection'. Bandan means 'to tie'. Thus it is a tie of protection and symbolises the bonds of loyalty and friendship. **Raksha Bandan** shows the duty of the brother to protect

▲ This Hindu boy and girl live in Britain. You can see the delight and pleasure in the girl's face as she ties the rakhi around her brother's wrist.

▲ An Indian girl looks at rakhis in a market in Chandigarh, India.

his sister from trouble and danger. In India, stalls appear everywhere selling rakhis and in Britain brothers receive them as gifts through the post and proudly display them to show how much they are loved by their sisters. Women without brothers tie the rakhi on men who regard them as sisters. It both shows the respect of the man for the woman and is a universal symbol of brotherhood and sisterhood. Friends might also exchange friendship bands.

Navaratri, Durga Puja and Dusserah

This important festival celebrates the awesome power of the goddess to protect everyone from harm and evil. It falls in the Hindu month of Ashwin, during the autumn, a time of change and astrological significance.

Navaratri means nine days and so devotion to the goddess continues for nine 'divine' nights, then on the tenth day, which is considered the victory day or **Dusserah**, the victory over the various demons, depending on the story being used, is celebrated.

During this festival the goddess is worshipped in three different forms. The first three days are dedicated to Durga (**Durga Puja**), who has the power to destroy all vices and shortcomings, the next three days are dedicated to Lakshmi, who can bestow wealth, and the last three days are dedicated to Sarawati, who can bring wisdom and success in life.

In some households, a special shrine is made for the image of the goddess and puja is performed twice a day. An oil lamp is lit and kept burning for nine days. Each day, garlands of flowers are hung above the image.

In the east of India, in West Bengal, Durga is favoured and huge Durga images are made and paraded through the streets. On the tenth day the story celebrating Durga's annihilation of the demon Mahishasura is re-enacted with public gatherings, fireworks and the burning of effigies of the demon.

▲ Hindus performing a danga ras (stick dance) during a Durga festival.

▲ The burning of an image of Ravanna, in Leicester.

In the west of India, in the state of Gujarat, the mother goddess (Mataji) is worshipped. Here, women follow the custom of painting brightly coloured pots, each containing water, to represent the changing world, and a lamp to represent the eternal light of God.

All over India women celebrate this special time by buying gold jewellery and wearing elaborate clothes for the pujas and nightly dancing.

This festival is famous for the special dances that are performed by the women in the evening at the mandir. They are called garba (circle dances) and danga ras (stick dances). It is said that the women are like the gopis or milkmaids who danced all night with their beloved Krishna, and sometimes young girls are dressed up and honoured as if they are goddesses.

In Britain, this festival is very important to Hindus from Gujarat and sometimes special halls are hired to make sure there is room for all the dancing.

In some parts of India, the tenth day (Dusserah) is celebrated with public gatherings and fireworks, in which large figures of the demon **Ravanna**, made from bamboo and paper, are eventually blown up or set on fire to show the overcoming of evil by the gods.

'Why mother not father you may ask. Let me just say that we believe that God's glory, his cosmic energy, can best be shown as the motherhood aspect of God. Just as a child finds everything it needs in its mother, so all of us look on God as mother. In fact Hinduism is the only religion in the world which gives so much importance to the mother aspect of God.'

A Hindu on
www.hinduism.about.com/library

TEST YOURSELF

A B C What is the meaning of each of the following features of Navaratri: durga, puja, garba, danga ras?

DIVALI

Divali is the best known of all Hindu festivals. It begins at the dark end of one month, Asvina (October), and ends at the new moon at the beginning of the next month, Karttik (November). The name of the festival means 'cluster of lights', and refers to the clay lamps that are placed both inside and outside every home and temple. They relate to the story of Rama and Sita, who needed a row of lights to guide them on their journey to their home city of **Ayodhya**, after their victory over the demon king Ravanna. In Britain and India, Hindus decorate their homes and public buildings with many brightly coloured lights. The house is cleaned especially and the pavements are covered in drawings, called **rangoli** patterns, which are made with brightly coloured chalks. New clothes are worn and presents are given out.

▲ A doorway decorated with a rangoli pattern in Rajasthan, India. Rice powder was used for this one, marking the first day of the Divali festival.

Divali also marks the beginning of the new year for Hindus so it is regarded as a good day to sort out business accounts, settle all debts and start new accounts. There is a special puja in the mandir for businessmen, who make offerings to Ganesha for good luck. There is also special puja for Lakshmi, the goddess of wealth. Some Hindu children believe that the goddess Lakshmi, guided by lamps, visits the homes of good children and leaves gifts for them.

The religious meaning of Divali is the triumph of good over evil, the coming of light or wisdom into the darkness of evil and ignorance, and the opportunity to make a new start in all aspects of life. The story of Rama and Sita from the Ramayana is often retold at Divali in films and dramas.

▲ Account books are blessed during Divali.

The story of Divali

Many years ago in India there lived a king called Dasratha who ruled in Ayodhya. He had three wives and four sons. The eldest, Rama, was heir to the throne but was also the god Vishnu in human form. Queen Kaikeyi, Rama's step-mother and Dasratha's favourite wife, was jealous because Rama was to become king and she wanted her own son to inherit the kingdom. So she told her husband lies about Rama, with the result that Dasratha banished Rama from his kingdom and sent him into exile for 14 years.

A New Approach – Hinduism

Rama had a beautiful wife, Sita, who insisted on going into exile with him, along with his brother Lakshmana. They all lived in the forest, but one day while Rama and Lakshmana were out hunting, the demon king Ravanna changed himself into a deer and tricked Sita into leaving her protected place in the forest. He kidnapped her and took her away to the island of Sri Lanka. When the brothers found out what had happened they were determined to rescue Sita. Hanuman, the monkey king, who was utterly devoted to Rama, came to their aid. With all of the monkeys in the forest, they were able to build a bridge over the sea to Sri Lanka.

After ten days of fierce fighting, they finally killed the demon Ravanna. Sita was reunited with her husband and they returned to Ayodhya now that their exile was over. The people of the kingdom lit divas all along the way so they could find their way back home.

TASK

a) Why is Navaratri so popular with women?
b) Why is it important to have a festival especially for the goddesses?

1 a) Choose two of the following festivals:

- Holi
- Divali
- Raksha Bandan
- Navaratri

(i)   Describe the main things Hindus might do during these festivals.

(10 marks)

(ii) Explain the religious meaning of these two festivals.   (8 marks)

b) 'Hindu festivals are really social celebrations rather than religious occasions.'

To what extent to you agree with this view? Give reasons for your answer.

(6 marks)

Assignment

REMEMBER

▶ The festival of Holi celebrates the coming of spring and hope for a good year ahead.
▶ Raksha Bandan celebrates the brother–sister bond.
▶ Navaratri, Durga Puja and Dusserah is a festival to celebrate the goddess and her power to protect from good and evil. She is worshipped in three forms: Durga, Lakshmi and Saraswati.
▶ Divali is the festival of lights, which celebrates the story of Rama and Sita.

WEBLINKS

Find out more details of Hindu festivals from all of these websites.

⚜ http://www.ahmedabadcity. com/tourism/html/festiv.html
⚜ http://www.hindunet.org/ festivals/
⚜ http://www.saranam.com/ Festivals/default.asp
⚜ http://www.iskcon.org.uk/ ies/festival.html
⚜ http://hinduism.about.com/

5

KEY WORDS

Bhagavad Gita: the most popular Hindu scripture; it is a section of the Mahabharata that presents the teachings of Lord Krishna.

Mahabharata: a popular scripture that is a long epic poem containing the great story (Maha) of India (Bharat).

Puranas: a collection of legends and myths about the popular deities.

Ramayana: another popular epic poem that contains stories that explain the moral and spiritual teachings of Hinduism.

Shruti: ancient and divine truths, not of human origin; these are directly heard and received by wise and holy men.

Smriti: truths that deserve to be remembered, but which are of human origin.

Upanishads: scriptures explaining the teachings of the Vedas that are communicated by gurus.

Vedas: the most ancient and important of the teachings of Hinduism.

THE VEDAS

The most important scriptures of the Hindus are known as the **Vedas**. These are regarded as the oldest scriptures in the world. They are still used today for ritual ceremonies and as a source of great wisdom and truth.

Hinduism teaches that the truths of the Vedas were first revealed by God at the beginning of time for the benefit of humankind. They are

▲ This is an orthodox Brahmin priest performing daily puja in front of a family temple in Kerala, India. In the photo you can see a stand used to hold the Vedas. The Vedas are written in Sanskrit and only the 'twice born' upper castes are considered pure enough to read them. It is the duty of Brahmins to know the scriptures and to explain them to others.

timeless and eternal truths. The earliest part of the Vedas is the ancient hymns of the Aryans who composed their hymns to their gods more than 3500 years ago. They were learnt by heart and passed down by word of mouth through the priestly castes. They are called **shruti** texts because they are not regarded as being of human origin but to have been revealed by Brahma, the creator god, to inspire the ancient seers or wise men. The wise men heard the scriptures and this is why the first Hindu scriptures are shruti, which means 'heard'. Shruti scriptures have more authority than later scriptures, called **smriti**, which translates as 'remembered truths'.

The word Veda means 'to know' and although the Vedas are very ancient, they contain a wealth of knowledge about art, medicine, mathematics, science and philosophy. The hymns of the Vedas are very beautiful and they describe the beauty of the dawn, the wonders of the world, and the journey of the soul through life, as well as

scientific theories. Passages from these Vedas form the basis for religious rituals performed by Brahmin priests for both temple worship and domestic ceremonies, such as rites of passage.

UPANISHADS

The **Upanishad** scriptures explain the Vedas and have a very special status due to their revealing of sacred truths in philosophical formulas. The word Upanishad is derived from the Sanskrit root 'shad', meaning 'to sit', and from the prefixes 'upa', meaning 'near' and 'ni', meaning 'down'. So, the seeker of enlightenment approached a teacher, sat down at his feet, settled his mind and listened very carefully to his spiritual instructions. These teachings are only meant to be heard by selected pupils who are dedicated to the pursuit of truth with their chosen guru or teacher. These scriptures have survived in their present form for at least 3000

▲ This photograph shows a small, street shrine (in Nepal), in which the scriptures (Vedas) are the object of devotion as well as the source of prayer and ritual. It is probably the place of a sadhu who has been left offerings of money to support himself in return for his teachings based on the scriptures.

A New Approach – Hinduism

▲ These men are reading the Upanishad scriptures in a temple in India.

both Hindus and people from the West. In Britain today, swamis from India are welcomed at Hindu community centres and mandirs to give talks on Hindu scriptures.

Gurus are essentially teachers of scriptures and may even be an older family member renowned for their wisdom and understanding who can offer advice and guidance. Sometimes, individuals will take time out from work and worldly responsibilities and search for their own particular guru and develop a special devotion to them. The person might submit to their guru's spiritual instruction for a period of time before returning to their everyday life.

Swamis are often very learned men who have studied the scriptures and developed their spiritual practice to a very high level. Some have set up ashrams or retreat houses that develop into colleges or universities where people can stay to study religious philosophy and meditation for a period of time. Sometimes, these swamis are invited to the UK to do lecture tours.

years. There are 13 major Upanishads and they teach about the inner self of man, the nature of Brahman, origin of the universe and the ultimate goal of liberation of the soul. They are as relevant and inspiring today as they were when they were first compiled, and many famous Western writers and philosophers have marvelled at the truths contained within them. These truths are expressed in poetry and you need to use intuition and imagination to appreciate them.

The main occupation of Indian holy men, especially the gurus, sannyasins and swamis, is to study and explain these teachings to those who seek spiritual guidance. Hindus might visit these swamis when they give audience in either holy cities or places of pilgrimage or in their own ashrams. Ashrams are retreat centres where people stay for a while to receive instruction and guidance from their guru. Some of these gurus and swamis are very popular and famous all over the world and receive a lot of attention from

▲ A Hindu swami, surrounded by things that have great importance and symbolic meaning for him.

▲ A guru.

▲ A sannyasin – a wandering holy man.

Sannyasins are individuals who leave their worldly responsibilities behind completely. They are wandering holy men seeking their own spiritual enlightenment, but who may sometimes offer some words of wisdom to those who support them in their homeless life.

MAHABHARATA AND RAMAYANA

The great Hindu epics – the **Mahabharata** and the **Ramayana** – belong to smriti scriptures. This means that the teachings are remembered rather than directly revealed to the listener, and these writings are well known by all Hindus. Unlike the Vedas, which are considered to be of divine origin, the smritis are of human origin and guide individuals in their daily conduct. They list the codes and rules governing the actions of the individual, community, society and nation.

The epics and stories are a way in which the ideals and values of the Hindu way of life are communicated to all Hindus, regardless of social background and education. Today they are greatly enjoyed by Hindus through the medium of cinema and television.

The Mahabharata was composed about 900 BCE, but was added to and amended over the next 600–700 years. Its title means 'great epic of the Bharats'. Bharat is sometimes the name given by the Indian people to their country. It has 200,000 verses and is thus the world's longest poem. Hindus regard the great sage Vyasa to be the author of this epic.

The epic deals with a power struggle between two royal families that represent the good forces (the Pandavas) and the evil forces (the Kauravas). The scene is the kingdom of the Kurus near modern-day Delhi. The conflict arose because the right to the throne was in dispute. The father of the Kuru princes was the eldest brother but he was blind, and so his younger brother Pandu became king. However, King Pandu retired to the forest to live as a sannyasin, leaving the throne to his brother Dhritarashtra. Dhritarashtra took his nephews into his household and treated them as his own sons. But his own sons became jealous of their cousins and resolved to murder them by setting fire to the

A New Approach – Hinduism

▲ A fresco depicting a battle scene from the Ramayana. Hanuman the monkey god leads his army in a battle against the evil Ravanna and his guards in an effort to release Sita from captivity.

house in which they were living. The five Pandava brothers heard of the plot in time to escape to the forest where they lived in disguise, far away from the capital. The greatest warrior and most skilled archer among the Pandavas was Arjuna who won a beautiful princess as the prize in an archery contest. In the meantime, the blind king decided to give back half of his kingdom to the exiled Pandava brothers. When the Kurus heard that the Pandavas were still alive, had a royal princess among them and ruled half of the kingdom from a new capital, they challenged their cousins to a gambling match.

The Pandava brothers were given loaded dice and so were tricked by the Kauravas into losing their kingdom again. They were banished to the forest for 13 years. When they returned to claim their rightful kingdom, their cousins refused to give it back. An enormous battle raged for 18 years in which the Kuru brothers and their huge army were totally destroyed. The Pandava ruled the kingdom righteously and then retired from worldly activities to the mountains of the Himalayas to complete the fourth stage of life and prepare for the final liberation of the soul and union with God.

THE BHAGAVAD GITA

The word Gita means 'song' and Bhagavad refers to 'Lord', so **Bhavagad Gita** means 'Song of the Lord'. It is a section of the Mahabharata and is the most famous and well known of all Hindu scriptures. It is included in the sixth book of the Mahabharata, although it was probably written much later, in the third century BCE. It has been the inspiration for many great thinkers, as well as ordinary folk, and has been called the jewel of ancient India's spiritual wisdom.

The story starts with Arjuna preparing to fight his cousins in the terrible war. As the armies line up for battle at a place called Kurukshetra he is struck with horror at the prospect of killing his kin. He orders his chariot to withdraw and is

▲ This carved stone frieze at Ellora tells the story of the Mahabharata.

then given advice by his charioteer, who is in fact Lord Krishna, an avatar of the god Vishnu, in disguise. The special message of the Gita is that devotion to God with complete surrender and trust is the highest form of worship and a means to attaining the highest goal of moksha. Moksha, a spiritual state of great happiness and wisdom, can be attained through bhakti yoga. The Gita also teaches the way of karma yoga, which is a way of fulfilling one's moral duties without the desire for reward.

The Gita gives a unique insight into the Hindu vision of the nature of God in chapter 11, verses 9–14.

> The great lord of power and yoga revealed to the son of Pandu his all highest form.
> A form with many a mouth and eye and countless marvellous aspects
> Many indeed were its divine adornments, many the celestial weapons raised on high.
> Garlands and celestial robes he wore, fragrance divine was his anointing.
> Behold this God whose every mark spells wonder.
> The infinite facing in all directions
> If in a bright heaven there should arise the light of a thousand suns then they would resemble this wondrous lord.
> Arjuna then saw the whole wide universe in One converged.
> There he saw the body of the God of gods yet divided out in may forms.
> Then filled with amazement his hair standing on end Arjuna joined his hands in reverent greeting and bowed down before his lord.
>
> *Bhagavad Gita, Chapter 11, verses ix–xiv*

▲ The Bhagavad Gita in Sanskrit and English.

This love for a personal god is the reason why the Bhagavad Gita is so popular. It is available to everyone, not just learned priests and sannyasins who have turned away from the world. The Gita offers a way to liberation through the love of God and so is open to all people regardless of age, caste, sex or social standing.

RAMAYANA

The Ramayana is shorter than the Mahabharata and is believed to have been written by Valmiki between 200 BCE and 200 CE, though it had been recited orally for many centuries before that. The message of this scripture is the triumph of good over evil and is the story of Rama and Sita as told at Divali. It shows Rama as an ideal son, student, brother, husband and king. Sita is the ideal Indian woman – wifely, faithful and possessing motherly courage in adversity.

So, these great epics are moral guides to the Hindu way of life.

PERSPECTIVES

Perspectives from a leading Hindu in Britain:

'The Ramayana has been from time immemorial a source of guidance, instruction and solace to many Hindus in India and throughout the world. It is very popular with Hindus who, on certain occasions in the year, listen to an uninterrupted reading of the whole epic. The Ramayana features a world of ideal characters, Rama, Sita, Lakshmana, Hanuman and Bharata. For countless centuries this epic has influenced Hindu religion and society, and has inspired family and social life.'

Explaining the Hindu Dharma, page 134

▲ This person is taking the role of Hanuman in a re-enactment of stories from the Ramayana.

▲ Many of the great stories of Hindu literature are available in the form of comic strips, which are extremely popular.

PURANAS

The **puranas** are a form of popular religious literature containing stories about the Hindu deities that help ordinary people relate to the main Hindu gods Vishnu, Shiva and Brahma. There are later Indian scriptures composed between the sixth and sixteenth centuries CE. In these stories the sages used the lives of saints and kings, and historical events, to explain the eternal teachings of Hinduism to the masses. The most widely known and read purana is the Bhagavad Purana, which contains a biography of Krishna. The stories show Krishna's powers as an avatar of Vishnu and some Hindus regard the stories as true events, while others use them to focus their loving devotion on Krishna.

The stories of Krishna's life reveal his miraculous feats in protecting the villagers from the disasters of floods and, wherever his influence was felt or experienced, there was peace, harmony, goodness and happiness.

Thousands of years ago King Ugrasena ruled the city of Mathura in northern India. He was gentle by nature but his son Kansa was a cruel tyrant, and even put his own father in prison. Kansa was warned by the gods that the eighth baby born to his sister Deviki would kill him, so he killed all of Deviki's babies, thus proving his wickedness. When she gave birth to her eighth son, Deviki's husband Vasudeva resolved to save him. Although the palace was heavily guarded he made a miraculous escape to a village called Gokul where he left the baby child Krishna with a cowherd Nanda and his wife Yashoda. Despite these attempts Kansa found out that the baby was still alive and sent various assassins to kill him.

These stories illustrate the Hindu belief that God takes many forms and intervenes in human affairs to ensure the well-being and progress of humankind, and the protection of dharma.

▲ The Bhagavad Purana.

TEST YOURSELF

1 Name the various kinds of Hindu scriptures.
2 What are the main themes of the Mahabharata and Ramayana?
3 What is the difference between shruti and smriti?

TASK BOX

a) Why are the Vedas the most sacred of scriptures for Hindus?

b) Why are the most popular scriptures in story form?

c) Why are these epics so popular with some Hindus?

d) Why are there so many different kinds of scriptures in Hinduism?

e) Discuss why some people place their trust in scriptures to guide them in their life and help them get closer to the truth.

1 What kinds of teachings are found in the following Hindu scriptures: the Rig Veda, the Upanishads, the Epics? (9 marks)

2 Explain the purpose of each of these scriptures within the Hindu tradition. (6 marks)

3 'Scriptures can never be as important as personal experience in coming to know the reality of God.'

Do you think a Hindu would agree or disagree with this statement? Give reasons for your answer. (8 marks)

Assignment

WEBLINKS

⊛ http://www.atributeto hinduism.com/Nature_ Worship.htm
Find quotes from the scriptures.

⊛ http://www.bbc.co.uk/ worldservice/people/ features/world_religions/ hinduism_prac.shtml

⊛ http://www.pearls.org/
Do a search for 'Hinduism'.

⊛ http://www.hindunet.org/ scriptures/index.htm

⊛ http://www.goloka.com/ index.html
Find pictures of the Ramayana.

⊛ http://www.hinduism.fsnet. co.uk/schools1p4.htm
Find passages from the Vedas, Upanishads and epics.

⊛ http://www.hinduismtoday. com/archives/2001/5-6/ 45_ insight.shtml
Find articles about Hindu scriptures by writing 'scripture' in the search box.

REMEMBER

▶ The Vedas are the most important teachings of Hinduism and are of divine making (shruti).

▶ The Upanishads are philosophical teachings explaining the Vedas.

▶ The epics Mahabharata and Ramayana are moral teachings and popular stories.

▶ Bhagavad Gita is the most well-known of all Hindu scriptures and is about devotion to Krishna.

▶ Puranas are popular stories about many gods.

6

KEY WORDS

Ahimsa: non-harm or non-violence.

Ayurvedic: a system of medicine based on natural principles.

Banyan tree: a sacred tree.

Chipko movement: an environmental movement dedicated to saving trees in India.

Goshalas: special places for the care of old animals, especially cows.

Mahatma Gandhi: important Indian leader in the twentieth century who preached the doctrine of ahimsa.

Nagas: mythical serpents who inhabit the oceans.

Peepul tree: the papal or fig tree considered sacred in India.

Sai Baba: a notable religious leader in India today.

Suti: the practice of a widow placing herself on her husband's funeral pyre (and being cremated with him).

Swaminarayan Hindu Mission: a movement within Hinduism based on the teachings of Swami Narayan.

Tulsi: a sacred herb, known as basil in Europe.

Vahana: a favourite animal or bird who acted as a vehicle for the gods.

KEY QUESTION

Why is life so sacred in Hinduism?

ISSUES OF LIFE AND DEATH

Hinduism teaches that God (Brahman) dwells within every living being, so Hindus have a great respect for all forms of life, be it human, animal or vegetable. Since many aspects of nature, such as the sun, moon, rivers, trees, mountains and plants are life-giving, they are sometimes worshipped as living deities.

> Brahman is the source of all beings, the seed of all things that are in this life have their life in Him. He is God hidden in all beings, their inmost soul. He lives in all things and watches all things.
>
> *Svetasvatara Upanishad Book 3, verse 7–9, (Zaehner)*

Most Hindus believe that God is in everything and that animals, as well humans, have souls and this produces an attitude of love and reverence for all forms of life. It is for this reason that many Hindus are vegetarian. Killing animals is against the principle of **ahimsa**, as Hinduism encourages total harmlessness to all living creatures.

Belief in reincarnation means that everyone is related to all living beings in some way. Your cat has been your brother in a previous life! Together with this belief, Hindus believe that all living beings can be seen as different forms of God, so they think that they should respect all beings, rich or poor, high or low caste, animal or human.

> A humble sage, by virtue of true knowledge, sees with equal vision a learned and gentle Brahmin, a cow, an elephant and an outcaste.
>
> *Bhagavad Gita, Chapter 5, verse xviii*

Mahatma Gandhi said that the duty of Hindus was to relieve the suffering of those less fortunate than themselves. He refused to accept that the outcastes were suffering on account of their past deeds. He called them 'Children of God' or Harijans.

Gandhi also campaigned for better rights for the untouchables. He went on hunger strike to bring their plight to public notice and also invited them to live in his ashram on an equal footing to all the other members, thus breaking down the boundaries between the castes.

A follower of Gandhi called Baba Amte lived and worked among the street people and shared with them the humiliation and degradation they experienced. He eventually founded a leprosy clinic in Nagpur.

In India, the **Sai Baba** movement has built many schools and hospitals where priority is given to the most needy people. The Sai Baba movement is now an international movement and in its special schools the aim is to enable all castes of children to live by the values of peace, non-violence, truth, right conduct and love.

▲ Baba Amte.

SUICIDE AND EUTHANASIA

The Hindu view of life is to encourage a positive attitude and accept the gift of life with gratitude. The Hindu teaching is that one has to use every opportunity in this life to create good karma and achieve a good rebirth. Committing suicide is not seen as a way of escaping from misfortune, but is only a way of increasing misfortune in the next existence. From the point of view of a doctor, helping in an act of euthanasia would bring them bad karma because they are separating the soul from the body before its natural time and disturbing the natural cycle of life and death and rebirth. Those interfering in this way would take on the remaining karma of the dying person. Suicide is a rejection of the gift of life so it is not accepted as a rightful act. However, it is not a taboo subject and the practice of suicide, as a religious act, is mentioned in the Ramayana and Mahabharata.

In the past, the practice of **suti** or suttee, when widows threw themselves onto the funeral pyre of their husband, was considered to be a noble act. However, this practice has now been abolished.

▲ Gandhi went on a hunger strike and nearly died to make his protests against injustice.

There is an accepted practice of prayopavesa, which is a fasting until death and is sometimes practised by elderly holy men and women as a courageous act. There are certain rules and conditions laid down to ensure it is a noble and dignified act. Within Hindu ethics and dharma, the taking of another person's life is a great sin and crime. Putting an end to someone's life by mercy killing is not acceptable either, but is sometimes practised, as it might be in any society. Some modern Hindu reformers have said that it can be a good deed to help end a painful life and therefore it is a moral obligation.

The whole approach to health and well-being in Hinduism is based on the ancient and effective principles of **Ayurvedic** medicine. This kind of treatment is not based on the same principles as medicine in the West, but is a kind of alternative medicine that treats the whole person, body, mind and soul, rather than just the physical symptoms. Many of the illnesses of the modern world, such as heart disease, cancer and ulcers, are due to stress, and Ayurvedic medicine provides spiritual remedies, such as prayer and meditation, as well as natural herbal remedies to restore health.

ABORTION

This would be against the Hindu belief of ahimsa or non-violence and Hindus are therefore opposed to taking a life in any form. It is believed that the foetus contains a soul (atman) and should be treated as a living being. The belief in reincarnation means that the life of an aborted foetus is cut short so it is deprived of the chance to improve its own destiny in its next life. Also, it will bring bad karmic results to the mother who aborts the foetus.

The classical texts, such as the Upanishads, are strongly opposed to abortion. They compare abortion to killing a priest, and a woman who aborts her foetus as losing her caste. In the Dharma shastras, moral codes which originated soon after 3000 BCE, it is seen as breach of duty for the householder to not produce children and continue the family.

However, India suffers greatly from the problems caused by over-population and abortion is widely used as a method of birth control.

Furthermore, abortion is used due to the cultural preference for sons and may be performed to prevent too many female babies being born.

The Hindu view is that life starts at the time of conception. This means that abortion does involve the taking of a life, and Hindus believe that this wrongdoing will bring its own inevitable consequences. However, compassion and understanding for this moral dilemma is expressed in some Hindu scriptures.

> When a person causes an abortion in pregnancy by striking, by medicine, or by annoyance, the highest, middle and lesser punishments shall be imposed.

From Kautilya's *Arthashastra, verse 229* (*Explaining Hindu Dharma*, page 169)

TEST YOURSELF

1 What is meant by ahimsa?
2 What does Hinduism teach about suicide, abortion and euthanasia?

TASK BOX

a) Explain why some Hindus might worship the sun, moon, rivers, trees and mountains.

b) Why is it considered wrong to carry out the acts of abortion, suicide and euthanasia?

c) Why do Hindus think it is wrong to kill any living being?

d) Discuss the following: 'Some people say this human life is a wonderful gift while others say it is a curse.'

e) Do you agree with the Hindu attitude towards euthanasia, suicide and abortion? What good reasons can you give to justify a person committing these acts?

RESPECT FOR THE ENVIRONMENT

Hindus regard the earth and their land as Mother Earth, and so respect and reverence for the natural world is part of Hindu thinking. The notion of ahimsa, combined with belief that God dwells in all forms of life, and the belief in rebirth, means that harming any living being is the same as harming one's friend or family. A Hindu saying is:

'The Earth is our mother and we are all her children.'

Hindu worship includes respect for mountains and rivers, as well as animals, plants and trees. From very ancient times, Hindus have regarded the whole universe as the dwelling place of God. The Bhagavad Gita expresses this very well.

I am the taste of water I am the light of the sun
I am the original fragrance of the earth
I am the heat in fire
I am the life of all that lives
Of lights I am the radiant sun
Among stars I am the moon
Of bodies of water I am the ocean
Of immovable things I am the Himalayas
Of trees I am the banyan tree
Of weapons I am the thunderbolt
Among beasts I am the lion
Of purifiers I am the wind
Of fishes I am the shark
Of flowing rivers I am the Ganges
Of seasons I am the flower bearing Spring
Of secret things I am the silence
Know that all opulent, beautiful and glorious creations spring but from a spark of my splendour.

Bhagavad Gita, Chapters 7 and 10

The care and protection of the environment by everyone is regarded as a religious duty in Hinduism, and the well-being of all mankind is seen as dependent upon proper and careful use of the natural resources. An article written in a special book to commemorate the opening of a new mandir in Manchester links modern ecology with ancient Hinduism:

PERSPECTIVES

'This concern with ecology is not new to Hinduism. It is because Hindu dharma teaches that nature is part of God's creation and gift for all living beings. The sun, the earth, the air and water are all worshipped and treated with great respect because without them we just cannot survive. Hindus believe that nature is like a mother who looks after all of us by providing food and nourishment. Just imagine what will happen to us if this earth and nature were to suddenly disappear. The importance of protecting the environment and ecology was appreciated by our Hindu ancestors thousands of years ago. In the most ancient scripture of the Hindus, the Rig Veda, it is written,

"Do not uproot the trees because they purify the environment."

What was taught by our ancestors is now being followed by the rest of the world.'

Murli Sthaapana, Gita Bhavan Hindu Temple Booklet

There have been several movements in recent years led by Hindus campaigning for and undertaking projects to preserve and protect the natural environment. Two movements have been founded by Sunderlal Bahuguna. One was founded to stop the construction of a dam at Tehri, which will devastate large areas of farming land, and the other is the **Chipko movement**, which aims to prevent further deforestation of the dense forests in the Himalayas. The Chipko movement uses a form of non-violent struggle as people link hands around trees to prevent them from being felled. The movement looks back to an incident in 1730 when tribal women in the state of Rajasthan embraced trees to prevent them from being felled for fuel by the Maharaja of Jodhpur. The women lost their lives as they were cut down with the trees. Their prayer was:

> You guard us, you feed us, you give us the breath of life.
> Tree, Give me your strength to protect you.

The BAPS Swaminarayan Sanstha (also known as the **Swaminarayan Hindu Mission** in the UK), besides providing schools and hospitals in India, has also built the largest temple outside India, in London. It was built using sound environmental principles – no steel or man-made materials were used – and it has energy-saving pumps and low-energy lights throughout. To compensate for the English oak used in the adjoining Hareli complex, 2300 saplings were planted in Devon, England.

These movements, and others like them, are increasingly important in India as, although 70 per cent of the population are still engaged in farming using traditional methods, the country is fast developing and there is much deforestation, industrialisation, and air and water pollution taking place.

▲ This school is in Ganad, Lakhtar, in Gujarat, India. It was built as part of the rehabilitation efforts of BAPS after the Gujarat earthquake in 2001. It was opened in May, 2002.

Attitudes towards animals and plants

Particular kinds of plants and animals are regarded as sacred because of their medicinal properties or association with the deities. The **tulsi**, or basil plant, is sacred to Vishnu, and the bilva or bel to Shiva. Devotees cultivate these plants and use their leaves in worship. The **peepul tree**, or sacred fig tree, has been worshipped for many years and was the tree under which the Buddha become enlightened. The **banyan tree**, whose branches form the roots for new growth, is also a sacred tree.

Animals and birds, such as the bull, tiger, mouse, peacock, eagle and swan, are used as vehicles (**vahana**) for the various deities. Tigers, peacocks and elephants are protected animals in India.

Monkeys are often treated as sacred animals as they are seen as relatives of Hanuman, the monkey god and loyal servant of Rama. The same is true of elephants because of the god Ganesha. Snakes are often looked upon as guardians of the land they live in and villagers will offer bowls of milk to them. **Nagas**, or large serpents, are more like mythical beasts and are seen as protective forces. They are portrayed as many-headed cobras sheltering the gods from any kind of harm. Shiva also has snakes and serpents twined around him both as protectors and as symbols of fertility.

▲ A Banyan tree.

▲ A Nagas.

The sacred cow

The most sacred animal to Hindus is the cow, and the reverence for it is an expression of gratitude for life. The cow is a great source of nourishment and giver of life in village India. Not only does the cow provide food through milk, butter and yoghurt, but the bullock is essential for drawing carts and ploughs, and the dung is valued as manure and fuel and also for plastering floors. The bull is the animal on which Shiva rides, and bulls are often dedicated to temples of Shiva as an act of piety or in fulfilment of a vow. Stories of Krishna show him milking cows and playing with them. So, for many reasons, the cow is deeply revered by devout Hindus. The killing of cows is banned in some Indian states today and there are special retirement homes for elderly animals, mainly cows, called **goshalas**.

> Taking what has not been given, injuring creatures without the sanction of the law … are declared to be wicked actions!
>
> *Laws of Manu, Chapter 5*

▲ A cow.

VEGETARIANISM

The main reasons for not eating beef are religious ones, and not eating meat at all is a clear sign of religious purity and caste status. There are many other good reasons for not eating meat given by the devotees of Krishna Consciousness (ISKCON).

■ Meat-eating is unhealthy because the meat may contain preservatives and poisons.

■ Meat arouses the passions of anger and sex.

■ The breath that utters the sacred mantras from the Vedas should not be contaminated.

■ A devotee will only eat food that has been first offered to Krishna, and in the Gita Krishna eats only fruit and vegetables.

■ It is a much better use of natural resources and helps to preserve the environment if people have a vegetable diet rather than cultivating pasture for animals.

■ If we needlessly kill animals we will have to be slaughtered and eaten in our next lives.

Not all Hindus are vegetarian and some will eat mutton and chicken. Sometimes, red foods such as beetroot, carrots, water melon and red wine are not eaten because they are the colour of blood.

TASK BOX

a) Why are many Hindus vegetarian?

b) Why is the cow a sacred animal in Hindusim?

c) Explain why many Hindus respect the forces of nature.

d) Provide some good arguments in favour of vegetarianism and also some arguments against it.

e) What can non-Hindus learn from Hinduism about respecting and protecting the environment?

f) Find out more about the Chipko movement from these websites:
■ http://edugreen.teri.res.in/explore/forestry/chipko.htm
■ www.saveourearth.co.uk. Look under Information.

g) What other examples are there in Hinduism of people or movements who aim to protect the environment?

h) Write about the achievements of the Chipko movement, especially the women's actions.

1 **a)** Explain the Hindu teaching on the sanctity of life with reference to the concepts of ahimsa and the eternal soul (atman). *(8 marks)*

b) What is the Hindu teaching on (i) euthanasia and (ii) abortion? *(8 marks)*

c) 'Ahimsa is an impossible ideal to achieve for Hindus living in the modern world.'

How far do you agree or disagree with this statement? Give reasons for your answer. *(6 marks)*

2 **a)** Explain why Hindus regard the natural world as sacred. *(6 marks)*

b) Why is vegetarianism so important in Hinduism? *(6 marks)*

c) Give examples of ways in which Hindus have attempted to protect the natural environment. *(8 marks)*

d) 'Attempts to protect the natural environment in India are doomed to failure in the modern world.'

Discuss how far you agree with this statement giving reasons for your point of view. *(8 marks)*

Assignment

REMEMBER

- Beliefs in ahimsa, atman and reincarnation influence ideas about the sacredness of life.
- The Hindu attitudes towards suicide and euthanasia vary and include that it is against the law of karma, and a moral duty.
- The practice of fasting until death is called prayopavesa.
- Hindus regard abortion as a sin but it is widely practised for practical reasons.
- Hindus regard earth as Mother Earth and respect it, thus there is great regard for the environment among Hindus.
- The cow is a sacred animal because of its association with stories about Krishna.
- Vegetarianism, or not eating meat, is a sign of religious purity and caste status.

WEBLINKS

- http://www.bbc.co.uk/religion/ethics/euthanasia/hindu.shtml
- http://www.atributeto hinduism.com/Nature_Worship.htm
  This website contains a lot of writing and pictures from various people showing how nature is worshipped within this tradition. Select some examples from this site that appeal to you.
- http://www.bbc.co.uk/schools/gcsebitesize/re/science/hicareofplanetrev2.shtml
  Find out about why Hindus take care of the environment.

7

KEY WORDS

Circumambulate: walk around the outside of a temple in a clockwise direction.

Gangotri: the source of the river Ganges in the Himalayas.

Hardwar: a holy city situated on the river Ganges.

Kailasha/Mount Meru: a sacred mountain in the Himalayas believed to be the dwelling place of the gods by some Hindus.

Kumbha Mela: a huge gathering of millions of pilgrims at Hardwar every 12 years for a special festival.

Rishikesh: a holy city on the banks of the river Ganges renowned for the ashrams of holy men.

River Ganges or Ganga: the largest and holiest river in India, considered to be the goddess Ganga.

Varanasi or Benares: a holy city on the banks of the river Ganges.

Vrindavan: some believe this is the birthplace of Krishna.

Yatra: Hindu word for pilgrimage.

KEY QUESTION

Why are certain places in India sacred and visited by many pilgrims?

All cultures have sacred places that have been visited for thousands of years due to their spiritual atmosphere and power. Some of these places are religious, as they are associated with the presence of God and significant events in the lives of prophets or saints. Others are famous for healing the body and mind. A pilgrimage is a journey to one of these sacred places.

India has many holy places and millions of Hindus from within India and throughout the world visit them. The word for pilgrimage in Hinduism is **yatra**. It is a religious act performed to experience the spiritual atmosphere of the sacred place and receive a spiritual benefit or blessing. Going on pilgrimage is not like going on holiday, it is meant to involve some self-sacrifice and physical hardship because it is an attempt to concentrate on spiritual life and leave the material world behind.

WHY DO HINDUS GO ON PILGRIMAGE?

Rivers are sacred places to Indians as they bring life-giving water to dry and barren areas. Just as water can wash away dirt, to some Hindus, bathing in a holy river can wash away the bad karma or sins of this life and past lives. So, the seven sacred rivers of India are all places of pilgrimage. Some Hindus go on pilgrimage to seek forgiveness of wrongdoing and will often choose to make their pilgrimage difficult and challenging, to make amends for their sins. They might measure their image in a series of prostrations as they **circumambulate** the temple to express this desire to do penance.

Some Hindus might go on pilgrimage to seek a cure for an illness and wish to ask the deity of that place to cure them. Often, it might be for the fulfilment of a vow or promise they may have made to their chosen deity when seeking some favour or blessing.

Another reason for going on pilgrimage is to seek spiritual liberation or moksha. This religious journey provides a unique opportunity to engage in some soul-searching, communicate with God and contemplate of the real purpose of life.

▲ Pilgrims journey towards a sacred place in Vrindavan, India, during Holi.

▼ These photographs (below and top right) show the many temples and ashrams that line the banks of the river Ganges at Varanasi. Each state in India has its own special ashram where pilgrims can stay free of charge. The many umbrellas mark the resting places of holy men who live by the river. Pilgrims walk down the steps (ghats) to bathe and perform puja.

WHERE ARE THE PLACES OF PILGRIMAGE?

One of the holiest places in India is the **river Ganges** and the city of **Varanasi** or **Benares** on its river banks. The Ganges is considered to be a living goddess and there are many stories and myths about it. Ganga, the river goddess, was reluctant to come down to Earth because her immense power would be too destructive. She only agreed to come when Shiva, who lives in the Himalayas, agreed to tie her down by using the locks of his hair.

Varanasi is also particularly associated with rites for the dead. Some Hindus go to the banks of the river to die and even ask to be lowered into the water so they can be in contact with it. Many Hindus are cremated on its banks. The ashes of those who die elsewhere may be sent to the Ganges or some other river to be scattered.

On the upper reaches of the river Ganges, the three sites of Badrinath, **Rishikesh** and **Hardwar** attract many pilgrims, despite the hardships of walking in the cold Himalayas. **Gangotri** is the source of the river high up in the Himalayas and the journey there is particularly arduous. Hindus believe that if a dying person sips the water from this source of the river their soul will be liberated. So, at certain times of the year, the sick and dying are carried on stretchers up to this special place where there are many shrines and dwelling places for sadhus and ascetics.

Hardwar is famous for the **Kumbha Mela** that takes places here every 12 years and lasts

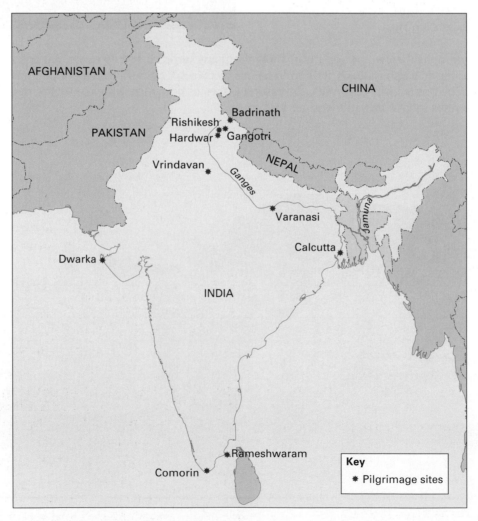

▲ Hindu pilgrimage sites in India.

▲ These sadhus are on a pilgrimage to Badrinath. They are preparing to go on the final phase of their journey to the source of the river Ganges. There can be considerable hardship and penance involved in going on a pilgrimage like this.

at least four days. It is in the Guinness Book of Records as the largest gathering in the world, with more than 30 million attending. This special gathering of pilgrims is based on a myth about a heavenly conflict among the gods, in which they fought over possession of a sacred nectar, amrit, which granted immortality. This fell to Earth in four different places, Hardwar being one of them. When certain astrological conditions prevail, the gathering (mela) takes place. Pilgrims engage in ritual bathing, religious discussions and assemblies. Many thousands of holy men and ascetics also gather and demonstrate their yogic powers.

Some pilgrimage places are on the sea. The most famous of these places is Dwarka, on the extreme tip of the state of Gujarat. This was seen as Krishna's capital city and celebrations of his birth and death take place there.

Comorin on the southern tip of India and Rameshwaram, which is between India and Sri Lanka, are famous because it is believed that Rama, Sita and Hanuman established two shrines to Shiva here. There are 32 wells here, one for each particular kind of sin.

Other pilgrimage sites are mountains, such as

Kailasha, also known as **Mount Meru**, high up in the Himalayan range. It is a very beautiful place and near to the sources of four of India's sacred rivers, including the Ganges and Indus.

Other sacred places are associated with particular deities and so Hindus will be attracted to those places belonging to their own personal deity. Shaivite Hindus who worship Shiva will visit Varanasi, while Hindus who worship Vishnu and his avatars will visit **Vrindavan**, where it is believed that Krishna played on the banks of the river Jamuna.

Other pilgrimage sites are based around important temples, such as the Mother Goddess temple to Kali in Calcutta, and the Vishnu temple at Badrinath, 915 metres (3000 feet) up in the Himalayas.

WHAT DO HINDUS DO ON PILGRIMAGE?

Pilgrimages are seen as important events in a Hindu's lifetime and they are carefully considered and planned. Pilgrims often make very long and arduous journeys to reach these sacred places and do so without many material comforts. They live in very basic accommodation when they get there.

At the pilgrimage sites, the pilgrims:

- perform puja and make offerings for their departed relatives (Shraddha rites)
- circumambulate the temples in a variety of ways, sometimes by prostrations
- view the image of the deity in the inner sanctum – the darshan
- often visit a family priest who offers advice and a sense of continuity as he and his forefathers may have been in touch with this family for generations.

TEST YOURSELF

1 Give four reasons why Hindus go on pilgrimage.
2 Why are some places sacred to Hindus?
3 Name four places of pilgrimage.

▲ The Fire Puja at Hardwar. This spectacular puja is performed for pilgrims at festival times. Fire is one of the basic elements of life, and is always used in puja.

▲ Vrindavan, on the banks of the Jamuna, is believed to be a place where Krishna spent his childhood and youth – where he played with the gopis (milkmaids) and saved villages from disaster. Devotees of Krishna are filled with joy when they see this place.

A New Approach – Hinduism

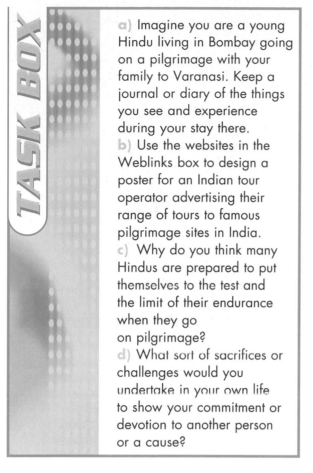

TASK BOX

a) Imagine you are a young Hindu living in Bombay going on a pilgrimage with your family to Varanasi. Keep a journal or diary of the things you see and experience during your stay there.

b) Use the websites in the Weblinks box to design a poster for an Indian tour operator advertising their range of tours to famous pilgrimage sites in India.

c) Why do you think many Hindus are prepared to put themselves to the test and the limit of their endurance when they go on pilgrimage?

d) What sort of sacrifices or challenges would you undertake in your own life to show your commitment or devotion to another person or a cause?

WEBLINKS

- http://www.ahmedabadcity.com/tourism/html/festiv.html
- http://www.pilgrimage-india.com/hindu-pilgrimage/
- http://www.all-indiatravel.com/hindu-pilgrimage-india/
- http://www.indiaoz.com.au/hinduism/articles/cows.shtml

Find out about Varanasi, Hardwor, Rishikesh, Dwarka and Vrindavan. Then write a journal of an imaginary visit to these places.

REMEMBER

- Hindus go on pilgrimage to try to wash away the bad karma of their previous lives.
- Places of pilgrimage are: river Ganges, Varanasi, Hardwar, Kumbha Mela, Dwarka, Comorin, Kailasha and Vrindavan.

---

1 a) What might Hindus do on pilgrimage? (6 marks)

b) Choose two places of pilgrimage for Hindus and explain why they are places of pilgrimage. (6 marks)

c) 'Pilgrimage is not essential to the Hindu's way of life.'

Do you agree or disagree with this statement? Give reasons showing you have considered another point of view. (6 marks)

Assignment

UNIT EIGHT | Moral Issues

8

KEY WORDS

Arjuna: the hero in the Gita.

Artha: wealth or advantage.

Artha shastras: a Sanskrit text dealing with worldly matters, wealth and monarchy.

Atithi: unexpected guest.

Bhoodan movement: a movement aiming to redistribute land so rural Indians can make a decent living.

Indira Gandhi: a former female prime minister of India.

Laws of Manu: a code of law books complied in the period between 200 BCE and 200 CE exploring the correct practices for each caste and stage of life.

Ram Mohun Roy: a Hindu reformer (1772–1833).

Satya: truthfulness.

Satyagraha: soul force not body force.

Shanti: a Sanskrit word meaning 'peace'.

Suti or sutee: the practice of a widow burning herself to death on her husband's funeral pyre.

Vinoba Bhave: a follower of Gandhi who founded organisations to help the poor.

KEY QUESTION

How does Hinduism encourage equal rights for women?

THE ROLE OF WOMEN

The role of a woman as a mother has always been given very high status in Hinduism. Everything good, blissful, protective and evil-destroying is associated with the mother goddess. Mother worship is very much part of Hinduism, as the mother is the first teacher of the child. However, there are different attitudes and opinions about the role of women.

Some Hindus have very traditional views about women and family life, and think that women should be homemakers and accept the authority of their husband. Others are more open-minded and believe that there should be equality for men and women.

Some aspects of Hindu life give men greater importance than women, for example:

- only men may act as priests at religious rituals
- only sons can perform funeral rites
- only boys receive a sacred thread in the upanaya ceremony.

However, attitudes towards women have changed in the past 50 years and it is now acceptable and achievable for women to have equal social status with and enjoying the same success as men.

PERSPECTIVES

Indira Gandhi was a very strong, courageous and highly respected prime minister in recent times. After India's independence in 1947 women were given equality before the law and equal voting rights. Also, some of the modern movements in India asserted the rights of women to education and careers.

Widowhood

In the past, it was customary for a woman only to have one husband in her lifetime, whereas men were allowed to remarry. Since many women were married at a young age to older men, they were often widowed while they were still young women in their thirties. This was seen as a miserable fate because a widow remained entirely dependent upon her husband's family and was expected to lead a very simple life wearing plain clothes with no adornments, and experience little enjoyment of life. They had no education, no money and no social standing, and were sometimes forced to remain unpaid house-maids in their husband's families. In the past, young widows from high caste families burned themselves on their husband's funeral pyres. This was called **suti**. **Ram Mohun Roy**, a religious reformer, campaigned strongly against this practice, and it was abolished by law in 1829.

The Hindu Widow's Remarriage Act also changed the outlook for widows completely. (Until this act widows had been forbidden to remarry by law – they had no education, money or social standing.) Some social reformers in India set up special colleges for the education of widows. Today, the Women's University of Bombay is a flourishing institution that provides a range of qualifications for women who are actively involved in many projects for the improvement of social and economic conditions throughout India. The motto from this university is: 'An enlightened woman is a source of infinite power'.

▲ This is Professor Joglekar of the Women's University of Bombay. The university originated at the time of Ram Mohun Roy.

▲ Ram Mohun Roy, a religious reformer in the 1800s.

Women as wives and mothers

The more traditional view of the role of women is conveyed in this passage from the **Laws of Manu**.

> Where women are respected, there lives God. If the wife is obedient to the husband, and the husband loves his wife, if the children obey the parents, and guests are entertained; if family duties are performed and gifts are given to the needy, then there is Heaven and nowhere else.

Ethical Issues in Six Religious Traditions, page 17.

Just as Hindu deities are shown with male and female aspects intertwined, so a husband and wife are seen to depend upon each other. The wife is indispensable to her husband as his constant companion, sharing his joys and sorrows and assisting him in every way. In the home the woman is likened to the various goddesses. If she is like Lakshmi, she will bring peace, harmony and prosperity to the household; as Saraswati she gives knowledge, education and wisdom to her children. The goddess Sita is also a good role model for Hindu women. Sita, as Rama's wife, showed great character and faithfulness, and was willing to suffer hardship for her husband's sake.

All Hindu women will expect to get married. This important stage in her life is the fulfilment of her womanhood. The marriage is a religious ceremony and the woman takes a vow of service, devotion and undying faithfulness to her husband. She is expected always to honour and respect her husband and, on his death, never insult his name. Breaking the marriage vows through any kind of unfaithfulness would be socially unacceptable. Indian national law permits divorce but there are strong community pressures against it. A divorced woman will usually return to her parents or her brother and a second marriage arranged for her if possible.

As a wife and mother, the Hindu ideal is for a woman is to be utterly dedicated to her family and to bring the religious observance and devotion to the gods into the home. It is the women of the household who organise and perform daily puja.

The position of a Hindu woman in her husband's family is made secure when she becomes pregnant, especially with male children. Only then does she become a full family member. Also it is the tradition for the son to look after his mother in her old age so, with a son, her future is secured. Having a large family is a mark of prestige, especially if the children are sons. Girls are less popular since they cannot continue a family business but are destined to marry and serve their husband's family. Thus the birth of a girl is greeted with less joy in some families. As well as being a source of worry during the adolescence, girls are expensive, as the father has to provide a dowry for his daughter, which is given to her husband as part of the marriage arrangements. The larger the dowry, the more attractive she is. However, although the practice of giving a dowry has been abolished by law, it remains in common practice today.

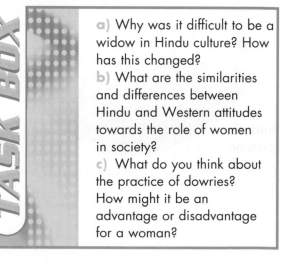

WAR AND PEACE

KEY QUESTION

What does Hinduism teach about non-violence and war?

Hinduism is quite famous for its teaching on non-violence. The concepts of **ahimsa** (non-violence) and **satya** (truthfulness) are the most basic and important moral principles for all Hindus, regardless of their caste or stage in life. Ahimsa means avoiding the harming of other living beings in any way and this belief has a long history in Hinduism. For centuries, the ideal of a peaceful life in harmony with nature, has been the goal of Hindus, rather than military strength and conquest. One writer has said that the reason why the Indian subcontinent was invaded throughout its history by tribes from outside India, like the Moguls, the European imperialists and the British, is that the Hindu kingdoms did not have a tradition of military fighting and so were vulnerable to invaders.

The Hindu attitude to war

In the Mahabharata, the Hindu attitude to war and peace is expressed in many of the stories. The most famous of these is **Arjuna**'s dilemma in the Bhagavad Gita. Arjuna is faced with the prospect of going into battle against his kinsmen, his cousins and teachers. He is appalled at the thought of the slaughter that will follow. However, Krishna gives him the advice that it is sometimes necessary to fight a just war to over-come evil forces that rise up in society. Krishna tells Arjuna that to fight for justice and truth is to fulfil the law of God. He argues from three points. Firstly, as a prince and soldier he has to fight for the good of his people. Secondly, he can only cause the death of men's bodies, he cannot hurt their souls. Thirdly, he is not fighting for personal gain but for the benefit of mankind. He must fight to the best of his ability without hatred or bitterness. This approach is an example of karma yoga.

The Bhagavad Gita highlights the conflict between ahimsa and the warrior's duty to fight in a war. The scripture teaches that it is right to go to war if the reason and motive are just, and if this duty has to be fulfilled. The Gita also shows how the contemplation of the issue of war and peace can bring a deeper understanding and appreciation of the meaning and purpose of human existence.

> Think of thy duty and do not hesitate. There is no greater good for a warrior than to fight in a just war. There is a war that opens the doors of heaven. Arjuna! Happy the warrior whose fate it is to fight such a war.
>
> Prepare for war with peace in thy soul. Be in peace in pleasure and in pain in gain and loss in victory and defeat. In this kind of peace there is no sin.

Bhagavad Gita, Chapter 2, verses xxxi–xxxiii (adapted from Hindu Scriptures)

▲ This man is a soldier and an officer, and is of the Kshatriya caste. As a Hindu soldier, how useful would you find the justifications for war in the Hindu stories?

The law books of Manu also provide some guidelines with regard to what is the right conduct in relation to war and peace. Here it states that a Kshatriya should always be prepared to fight in a just war and behave honourably. This means he should not kill anyone who has surrendered or joins his hands and asks for mercy, is asleep or disarmed, is an onlooker not involved in battle, is an enemy who is wounded, or women and children.

The Rig Veda also states that:

 The warrior should not poison the tip of his arrow, he must not attack the sick or old, a child, or a woman or from behind. These are sinful acts and lead to hell even if the warrior is the winner.

Rig Veda 6 – 75 – 15 (as translated in *Explaining Hindu Dharma*, page 178)

Hinduism and pacifism

Mahatma Gandhi is one of the most famous people in the world for his belief in and practice of non-violence and pacifism as a way of fighting a war against injustice. He was greatly inspired by the Bhagavad Gita and has been regarded as the greatest pacifist of all time. During his lifetime the British ruled India, and because the Indian people wanted to rule their own country there was a national movement for India's independence. At one time, Gandhi led this movement but strongly asserted that the Hindus would not take up arms against the British; they would make their demands in a peaceful, non-violent way. He believed that non-violence would soften the heart of the attacker. He developed the idea of soul force, or **satyagraha**, which is using the power of the mind and soul rather than fighting back with weapons. His followers were called satyaghrahis. Gandhi created an 'army' of 'satyagrahis', i.e. an army of men and women who used their soul force rather than physical force or violence to fight injustice.

These people gave up their normal lives to live in ashrams created by Gandhi to train in strengthening their spiritual will-power to resist violent attacks. This method became a very potent weapon and was successful in winning independence from British rule.

All Hindu prayers end with the repetition of the word **shanti**, which means peace. It is said three times, once for inner peace and freedom from worry, twice for freedom from pain and illness and three times for peace from war and natural disasters.

TEST YOURSELF

1 What are meant by ahimsa and satyagraha?
2 What is Arjuna's dilemma in the Gita?
3 What kind of arguments for the just war can be found in the Bhagavad Gita?

TASK BOX

Read the Perspectives box on the opposite page.

a) Why did Gandhi believe in non-violence? Was he successful in achieving his aims?

b) How far do you agree with the Hindu attitude to war and peace?

c) How might the teachings of the Rig Veda and the Laws of Manu be applied to modern warfare and the use of violence in any conflict situation?

'The principle of ahimsa does not include any evil thought, any unjustified haste, lies, hatred, ill-will towards anyone.'

Non-violence does not mean cowardice, as Gandhi himself proved when submitting to blows from the police and imprisonment.

'Ahimsa is not the way of the timid and cowardly. It is the way of the brave ready to face death. He who perishes with sword in his hand is no doubt brave but he who faces death without raising his little finger is braver.'

'Satyagraha. Its root meaning is holding onto truth. I have also called it love force or truth force. I have discovered that in applying satyagraha one cannot inflict violence on one's opponent but attempt to win them over by sympathy and patience. Satyagraha is gentle and patient. It must not be the result of anger or malice. It is the direct opposite of compulsion. It is the complete substitute for violence. Every satyagrahi must resist those laws which are unjust in order to bend the will of the government to the will of the people.'

The Selected works of Mahatma Gandhi, Vol IV

▲ The memorial to Gandhi in Raj Ghat Park in Delhi.

WEALTH AND POVERTY

What is the Hindu attitude to wealth and poverty?

One of the four aims in life is **artha**, the gaining of wealth by honest means. Hindu dharma encourages Hindus to earn money honestly and lawfully. In this way a man can provide for his wife, children and extended family.

Guidelines on artha were written by a sage called Kautilya, who lived in 300 BCE and wrote the **Artha shastras**. This scripture includes teachings about accounts, coinage, trade, commerce, the armed forces, weights and measures, agriculture, law, government and administration. One of the duties of a householder is to be generous and hospitable to guests. It is a long-standing custom that there must be a table left for **atithi**, the unexpected guest. No guest, no matter how lowly, should be turned away without food.

There is a great deal of extreme poverty in India, by the standards of the affluent Western world, and there are many reasons for this. It is fully admitted by many economists that the present-day problems were caused by the exploitation of India's resources by the European powers during their time of colonial expansion. Also, the explosion in the population growth rate means that current levels of food production cannot provide for the number of mouths it has to feed. However, India is also a rapidly developing country and its social and economic conditions are changing constantly. Thus there are some moral issues associated with wealth and poverty.

The Hindu scriptures state that a man may keep what he needs for himself, but he should not hoard more than he needs and so deny others what they truly need.

 Gifts should be given daily to worthy recipients, and especially so on special occasions. And if a man is asked, he should, in accordance with his means, make a donation that is pure because of his faith.

The Law Book of Yajnavalkya, verse 203 (Goodall, page 321)

 One may amass wealth with hundreds of hands but one should also distribute it with thousands of hands.

If someone keeps all that he accumulates for himself and does not give it to others the hoarded wealth will eventually prove to be the cause of ruin.

Artharav Veda 3, 24–5 (as translated in *Explaining Hindu Dharma*, page 173)

Vinoba Bhave was a follower of Gandhi who wanted land to be redistributed from the wealthiest to the poorest as a means of overcoming poverty. He did not oppose the secular law that allowed ownership of the land, but worked to persuade people to give some of their land away voluntarily. His **Bhoodan movement**, which began in 1948, organised the redistribution of four million acres of land within the first six years of operation.

There are many projects underway in India that are trying to reduce poverty through a variety of ways. Many of the educational and commercial projects, and rural development programmes, are financed by charities and aid programmes, rather than governmental support. Many Hindu temples organise aid projects, and there are countless organisations within India aimed at improving the plight of the poor and needy.

TASK BOX

a) What does Hinduism teach about the proper use of wealth and attitudes towards poverty?

b) Give an account of any movement that has aimed to alleviate poverty in India.

c) Discuss the following: 'The organisation of wealth and poverty has nothing to do with religion.'

1 a) What is the Hindu attitude to the role of women in society? (8 marks)

   b) Why is the mother regarded as so important in Hindu society? (6 marks)

   c) 'Women will never be regarded as highly as men in Hindu society.'

   Do you agree or disagree with this view. Give reasons for your answer.

   (6 marks)

2 a) What can be learnt from Hindu teachings about war and non-violence?

   (8 marks)

   b) What are the arguments for a just war found in the Gita? (6 marks)

   c) 'Non-violence will never be effective against a strong military power.'

   How far do you agree with this statement? Give reasons for your point of
   view, referring to the Hindu teachings in your answer. (6 marks)

Assignment

REMEMBER

- The role of motherhood has a very high status in Hinduism.
- Hinduism teaches its followers to avoid conflict and war and is famous for its teachings on non-violence.
- Gandhi is famous for his practice of pacifism as a way of fighting a war against injustice.
- Hinduism teaches that wealth should be gained honourably but that it should only meet a person's needs. Any surplus should be used to help others less fortunate.

WEBLINKS

Find out about the various movements dedicated to improving conditions for the poor and under-privileged in India. The following websites will be helpful:

- http://www.aidindia.net/projects.htm
- http://www.betterworldlinks.org/book10r.htm
- http://www.sathyasai.org/ Find out about the service projects undertaken by the Sai Baba organisation.

Key Words Glossary

ahimsa: non-harm or non-violence

Ambedkar: an important Indian politician 1891–1956 who ensured that the dalits were given equal and fair treatment

ananta: a huge sea serpent with many heads arising out of the ocean upon which Vishnu lies

Arjuna: the hero in the Gita

Artha shastras: a Sanskrit text dealing with worldly matters, wealth and monarchy

artha: wealth or advantage

arti: offerings of light to the deity

ashrama: stage in life

asteya: truthfulness and honesty

atithi: unexpected guest

atman: the inner spirit dwelling in every living being, including animals; it is the eternal, indestructible and perfect spirit in everyone

avatar: a god in human or animal form

Ayodhya: the city belonging to Rama referred to in the Divali story

Ayurvedic: a system of medicine based on natural principles

banyan tree: a sacred tree

Bhagavad Gita: an important and popular scripture for Hindus, which explains why God came to Earth in the form of Krishna; it is a section of the Mahabharata

Bhagavad Purana: stories about the main popular gods

bhajan: special song and hymn to God

bhakti: loving devotion to the deity; worshipping God with much love and often lots of singing and dancing

Bhoodan movement: a movement aiming to redistribute land so rural Indians can make a decent living

Brahma: the creator god

Brahman: the Hindu word for God, the ultimate being or life force and energy that creates the universe

Brahmin: priest/teacher

caste: social status, from birth

chakra: wheel or disc

Chipko movement: an environmental movement dedicated to saving trees in India

circumambulate: walk around the outside of a temple in a clockwise direction

Dalit: a person outside the caste system; untouchable

darshan: viewing with respect a holy image and receiving a divine blessing in return

deity: one of the many gods worshipped by Hindus

devas: minor gods or spirits that inhabit the natural world, rivers, trees – even a human being can become like a deva or perfect being; devas are often goddesses

devotee: one who is devoted to a god

dharma: right conduct

dharma shastras: the rules, laws and customs that explain the duties for each stage of life

Divali: festival of lights

Durga Puja and Dusserah: a ten-day festival in the month of Ahwin celebrating various events from the epics, the Ramayana and Mahabharata, but especially a goddess festival lasting for ten days

Ganesha: an elephant-headed god who brings good luck

Gangotri: the source of the river Ganges in the Himalayas

garbha-griha: the inner shrine or womb house, containing the image of the deity

gayatri mantra: a famous Hindu prayer usually chanted at puja

gopis: the milkmaids who worshipped Krishna

gopuram: large towers or gateways found in temples in southern India

goshalas: special places for the care of old animals, especially cows

Hanuman: divine powers in the form of the King of the Monkeys; as Rama's loyal and devoted companion he is sometimes worshipped as a god in his own right

Hardwar: a holy city situated on the river Ganges

Holi: the spring festival

Indira Gandhi: a former female prime minister of India

Jatakarma: birth ceremony

jati: particular occupation or job

Kailasha/Mount Meru: a sacred mountain in the Himalayas believed to be the dwelling place of the gods by some Hindus

karma: law of cause and effect; destiny

Kautilya: an Indian philosopher of the fourth century BCE

kirtan: devotional singing

Krishna: one of the most popular avatars of Vishnu who loves human beings

Kshatriya: warrior/ruler

Kumbha Mela: a huge gathering of millions of pilgrims at Hardwar every 12 years for a special festival

Laws of Manu: a code of law books complied in the period between 200 BCE and 200 CE exploring the correct practices for each caste and stage of life

lingum: the male sex organ; sometimes used as symbol for Shiva

Mahabharata: a popular scripture that is a long epic poem containing the great story (Maha) of India (Bharat)

Mahatma Gandhi: important Indian leader in the twentieth century who preached the doctrine of ahimsa

mandapa: the pillared hallway or passageway leading to the inner shrine

mantra: a repeated phrase or prayer used in religious rituals and meditation aimed at focusing the mind on god

meditation: the practice of stilling the mind and removing ordinary thoughts, developing deep concentration and wisdom through the power of the mind

moksha: final goal, when the soul is freed from the body and merges with God

Mundan or Choodakarma: ceremony marking a child's first haircut

murti: the image of the deity that has been installed in the shrine

nagas: mythical serpents who inhabit the oceans

Nataraja: lord of the dance and another name for Shiva

Navarati: festival for the goddess lasting nine days

Om: a sacred sound that represents the powers of Brahman or god, or the symbol of Hinduism

peepul tree: the papal or fig tree considered sacred in India

prashad: food that has been offered to the gods and then given out to the worshippers

puja: worship or paying respects to God or a chosen deity

Puranas: a collection of legends and myths about the popular deities

Radha: Krishna's most devoted follower and wife

rakhi: friendship band

Raksha Bandan: a festival celebrating family bonds and friendship through tying a special friendship band or bracelet around a brother's wrist

Ram Mohun Roy: a Hindu reformer (1772–1833)

Rama: another avatar of Vishnu who shows courage and goodness

Ramayana: another popular epic poem that contains stories that explain the moral and spiritual teachings of Hinduism

rangoli: special patterns made with coloured chalks and powders drawn on the floor

ratha-yatra: a large procession that takes place at festival times

Ravanna: demon king

Rig Veda: one of the books of the Vedas, the most ancient hymns of the Aryan tribes of India

Rishikesh: a holy city on the banks of the river Ganges renowned for the ashrams of holy men

river Ganges or Ganga: the largest and holiest river in India, considered to be the goddess Ganga

Sai Baba: a notable religious leader in India today

samskars: rites of passage that mark important stages in life; in Hinduism there are 16 samskars

sanatan dharma: eternal laws; universal principles of morality

sandalwood: sweet-smelling oil or incense used in puja

Sanskrit: the ancient language in which the Vedas are written

satyagraha: soul force not body force

satya: truthfulness

sauca: purity

shanti: a Sanskrit word meaning peace

shikhara: a tower or spire above the image of the deity inside the temple

Shiva: the destroyer and re-creator god

Shraddha rites: special rituals conducted for departed relatives 12 days after their death

shrine: a place set aside for puja with images of the deity, flowers and lights, and incense

shruti: ancient and divine truths, not of human origin; these are directly heard and received by wise and holy men

Shudra: manual worker

smriti: truths that deserve to be remembered, but which are of human origin

suti or sutee: the practice of a widow burning herself to death on her husband's funeral pyre (and being cremated with him)

Swaminarayan Hindu Mission: a movement within Hinduism based on the teachings of Swami Narayan

Trimurti: the three aspects of the ultimate being Brahman expressed as Brahma, Vishnu and Shiva; in other words three aspects of God in one God

tulsi: a sacred herb, known as basil in Europe

Upanayana: sacred thread ceremony for Hindu boys of higher castes during adolescence

Upanishads: scriptures explaining the teachings of the Vedas that are communicated by gurus

vahana: a favourite animal or bird who acted as a vehicle for the gods

Vaishya: merchant; trader

Varanasi or Benares: a holy city on the banks of the river Ganges

varna: colour or caste

varnashramadharma: rules and customs for each stage of life and each caste

Vedas: the most ancient and important of the sacred scriptures of Hinduism

Vinoba Bhave: a follower of Gandhi who founded organisations to help the poor

Vishnu: the preserver god

vivaha: marriage ceremony

Vrindavan: some believe this is the birthplace of Krishna

yajna: a ritual that involves a form of sacrifice

yatra: Hindu word for pilgrimage

A New Approach – Hinduism

INDEX

A New Approach – Hinduism